# 1 MONTH OF
# FREE
# READING

## at
## www.ForgottenBooks.com

By purchasing this book you are eligible for one month membership to ForgottenBooks.com, giving you unlimited access to our entire collection of over 1,000,000 titles via our web site and mobile apps.

To claim your free month visit:
www.forgottenbooks.com/free770793

\* Offer is valid for 45 days from date of purchase. Terms and conditions apply.

ISBN 978-0-483-42957-4
PIBN 10770793

This book is a reproduction of an important historical work. Forgotten Books uses state-of-the-art technology to digitally reconstruct the work, preserving the original format whilst repairing imperfections present in the aged copy. In rare cases, an imperfection in the original, such as a blemish or missing page, may be replicated in our edition. We do, however, repair the vast majority of imperfections successfully; any imperfections that remain are intentionally left to preserve the state of such historical works.

Forgotten Books is a registered trademark of FB &c Ltd.
Copyright © 2018 FB &c Ltd.
FB &c Ltd, Dalton House, 60 Windsor Avenue, London, SW19 2RR.
Company number 08720141. Registered in England and Wales.

For support please visit www.forgottenbooks.com

# LIVING AGE

FOUNDED 1844    BY E. LITTELL

Published under the auspices of
the Atlantic Monthly

## SATURDAY, DECEMBER 16, 1922

### CONTENTS

| | | |
|---|---|---:|
| A Week of the World | | 615 |
| Reparations in the French Chamber—A Farmers International—Joffe at Peking—Fascisti in Hungary and Bavaria—News Barriers in Europe—An Unpublished Crispi Anecdote | | |
| A Levy on Capital. *Arguments for and against This Solution of Europe's Debt Problem* | | 621 |
| Latin-American Revolutions | MANUEL UGARTE | 627 |
| *A Political Analysis and a Moral* | | |
| From Dublin to Kerry | E. S. G. | 633 |
| *An Irishwoman's Experience* | | |
| Bulgaria's Labor Army | NINO SALVANESCHI | 636 |
| *A New Phase of Compulsory Service* | | |
| Air Travel in Russia | GEORG POPOFF | 638 |
| A Christian Refuge and Islamic Ambitions | COLIN ROSS | 642 |
| *Glimpses of Asia's Ferment* | | |
| Rouget de Lisle and the Marseillaise | EDOUARD GACHOT | 647 |
| The Augustan Age of Science | SIR RICHARD GREGORY | 650 |
| Al Wasal, or The Merger | HILAIRE BELLOC | 658 |
| *An Arabian Nights Tale up-to-date* | | |
| In the Red Sea | MAJOR ARTHUR W. HOWLETT | 662 |
| Radha's Child | C. R. | 665 |
| *An Indian Anti-Caste Story* | | |
| A Page of Verse | | 668 |
| The Later Autumn—After Victor Hugo—Lover's Reply to Good Advice | | |
| Life, Letters, and the Arts | | 669 |
| A Nonsense Library—'L'Écho De France'—Vergil's Farm—The Rubaiyat of Two Modern Omars | | |
| Books Abroad | | 673 |

## THE LIVING AGE COMPANY

PUBLICATION OFFICE: RUMFORD BUILDING, CONCORD, N. H.

EDITORIAL OFFICE: 8 ARLINGTON STREET, BOSTON 17, MASS.

$5.00 a Year                                                             15c a Copy

*Entered as second-class mail matter at Concord, N. H.
Foreign Postage, $1.50; Canadian Postage, 50c*

*'Strong as man and tender as woman, books welcome you in every mood.'* — *Langford.*

# In Defence of Nonsense

SINCE their ennui troubles them more than their ignorance, people prefer being amused to being informed,' remarked L'Abbe Dubois in commenting disapprovingly upon the popularity of light fiction. Which, after all, seems a rather uncharitable viewpoint. Does an appreciation of, let us say, Walter Pater's jeweled passages preclude one's enjoyment of 'Gentle Julia?'

What is behind this fatal tendency which makes for the exclusion of so many factors which enrich life? There are people who can resist Charlie Chaplin. If Charlie Chaplin is not funny to you that is your misfortune not your fault. But if your reason for not reacting to this 'humorous poet who happens also to be a great actor,' as someone has described him, is that you have persuaded yourself that one of your dignity, taste and traditions could not possibly be amused by a slapstick comedian, then you are betraying lamentable symptoms of exclusionism which may eventually result in your approaching the melancholy condition of that Bostonian who when reproached for omitting to invite his brother to his housewarming replied that 'one must draw the line somewhere.'

Why exclude merely entertaining books? Eddie Foy is not comparable to Forbes Robertson but each has delighted us. There is little relation between George McManus and Frederick MacMonnies but we accept both gratefully. Then whence this confusion of thought about books? Because it is true, as Bartholin declaimed:

'Without books God is silent, justice dormant, natural science at a stand, philosophy lame, letters dumb and all things involved in Cimmerian darkness,' there exists in some quarters a prejudice against light reading.

Which seems about as logical as to condemn a bit of Haviland china because Rodin's medium was clay.

Ours is a sprightly, unpretentious age and though its frankness sometimes degenerates into flippancy, who would return to that Victorian dignity which sometimes perilously approached pomposity? It was with the completest understanding of how it would affect the erudite that Dr. Frank Crane remarked to the writer that with fifty years of reading behind him, he felt that in all literature the volume from which he had gained most intense pleasure was 'The Adventures of Sherlock Holmes.' Judged by the test of her contribution to the common sum of human happiness, it is altogether probable that the life of Anna Katharine Green was more significant than that of William Dean Howells. Nor is it necessary to justify light romances by Bernard Shaw's ingenious defence: that by indulging vicariously in duels, murders and deeds of violence one is relieved, according to Freud, of the impulse to punch one's neighbor's nose.

Many a t. b. m. has embarked upon an expensive foreign tour to rebuild shattered nerves when through the medium of a few dozen of the less weighty novels advertised in the *Atlantic* columns he might have set sail upon the magic sea of the novelist's imagination to achieve exactly the same result: a lift from the workaday world, complete relaxation, and resultant mental health, not to mention englamored hours of delightful entertainment. When you see a bookshop displaying the reproduced insignia, enter. For a two dollar bill the proprietor will sell you a ticket good for an eventful voyage 'on the foam, of perilous seas, in faery lands forlorn.' He sells the titles advertised in the *Atlantic*.

We sell Books advertised in THE ATLANTIC MONTHLY

---

THERE IS A BOOKSELLER IN YOUR TOWN

# This Week

An air-journey across Bolshevik Russia, with a narrow escape from death, is the substance of an experience that Georg Popoff relates in this issue of the LIVING AGE. The aeroplane was bound from Königsberg to Moscow and carried a package for Lenin, sealed with seven seals. Polish bullets and a crash to earth failed to prevent its arrival.

* * *

Reports of actual conditions in Central Asia are as rare as they are important. Colin Ross was lucky to emerge alive from that part of the world, and we are equally fortunate in being able to hear about his adventures and impressions of the trip. Bolshevik boy-scouts drilling under the shadow of Mount Ararat, side by side with British and American units is one of the more picturesque scenes.

* * *

From Dublin to Kerry is a less sensational but a no less interesting journey. The hopeless disorder of the country and the tragedy, lying so close behind the mask of unconcern, are vividly brought out by an Irish woman who has just been there herself.

* * *

The possibility of a capital tax in England has been increased by the large Labor vote in the recent elections. The subject is competently discussed, *pro* and *con*, by the *New Statesman* and the *Spectator*.

* * *

Business men have fought a little shy of South America, by reason of the frequent and devastating revolutions that take place there. Manuel Ugarte, one of the leading writers in that continent, believes in a great Latin American Union. He is thoroughly conversant with his subject and his opinions are sound as well as encouraging.

* * *

Bulgaria has set about her reconstruction work with admirable energy. Conscripting labor, rather than soldiers, is an example which has proved itself worthy of serious attention, and Communists may regard it as a triumph for their doctrine of working for the State.

* * *

The Marseillaise is generally considered the finest of all national anthems. The history of its author, which includes an account of how he composed the song, forms a vital part of the great tradition of French patriotism.

* * *

Readers of the LIVING AGE are already acquainted with Hillaire Belloc, who is at his best in an amusing description of a merger, in the city of the Caliphs. And Thomas Hardy needs even less introduction. His poem, on the Page of Verse, would be read if only because it is written by the greatest living figure in English letters.

*A Gift Book of Unusual Beauty*

# MEMORIES OF A HOSTESS
### *A Chronicle of Eminent Friendships*
DRAWN CHIEFLY FROM THE DIARIES OF MRS. JAMES T. FIELDS

### *By* M. A. DeWolfe Howe

*Turn these pages of happy reminiscence and you find yourself in the delightful old-time Boston of the Nineteenth Century*

Nothing could more eloquently suggest the Boston of other days than the reminiscent pages skilfully gathered by Mr. Howe out of Mrs. Fields's diaries and other papers. The period of their recollections is mainly the sixties and the seventies when Boston was a centre of American culture and literary life. There were giants in those days, and at least half the great figures of American letters and the learned professions either lived in Boston or had close association with it. Therefore the diaries of the gracious lady who was the wife of a leading publisher, editor, lecturer and writer are necessarily an intimate record of the place and the time.

The times have changed, but many of us have not changed with them. Neither have we lost our appreciation or our longing for those bygone days when Longfellow and Lowell and Holmes and the others were a part of Boston life, and when among its frequent distinguished visitors were Mark Twain and Edwin Booth and Joseph Jefferson. These are only a few of the names that throng the pages of Mrs. Fields's diaries as she records the comings and goings of their possessors through the hospitable doors of the Fields house.

Dickens, Hawthorne, Charles Sumner, Bret Harte, Ellen Terry, Christine Nilsson, the Henry Jameses, father and son, and a host of others cross Mrs. Fields's canvas. Many of the pen portraits are succinct and picturesque. Altogether it is a notable book of reminiscent literary biography.

—*Boston Transcript.*

*Illustrated with portraits and facsimile letters.* $4.00

### At All Booksellers, or THE ATLANTIC MONTHLY PRESS

---

THE ATLANTIC MONTHLY PRESS, Inc.   L.A. 12-16-22
8 Arlington Street, Boston (17), Mass.

*Gentlemen:* Enclosed find........and mail, postpaid,........copies
MEMORIES OF A HOSTESS

(If you wish this book sent direct, with Christmas card bearing your name as donor, kindly enclose detailed instructions.)

Name..........................................Address..............................

# THE LIVING AGE

### for NEXT WEEK

*WILL CONTAIN AMONG OTHER THINGS*

WHEN THE FRANC COLLAPSED — *William Bolitho*
*The Exchange Panic in Paris*

A FIVE YEARS' LESSON
*Contrasting Appraisals of the Russian Revolution*

AN AUTUMN VISIT TO BAVARIA — *Auriol Barran*

FUNDAMENTALS OF POLISH POLICY — *A Warsaw Correspondent*
*The Last Election Issues*

REMOTER RUSSIA. *A Snapshot of a Land of Graft* — *Georg Cleinow*

A MEXICAN LANDSCAPE — *Gabriela Mistral*

THE LONG JOURNEY. *A Vision of Pre-human History*
— *Johannes V. Jensen*

WAGNER RECONSIDERED — *Louis N. Parker*

CHRISTMAS CAKES AND CHRISTMAS PARTIES
— *J. Fairfax-Blakeborough*

ON CAROLS — *R. L. G.*

DULLNESS: A LIVELY DISSERTATION — *George Saintsbury*

If you are not a subscriber, and would like to receive
the magazine regularly, fill out the coupon below

---

THE LIVING AGE
Rumford Building, Concord, N. H., or
8 Arlington Street, Boston (17), Mass.

*Gentlemen:* Enclosed find $5.00 for my subscription to the LIVING AGE for one
year beginning..................................................................................................

*Name*..............................................................................................................

*Address*.................................................*City*..............................................

12-16-22

## Babbitt
*By* SINCLAIR LEWIS
Author of *Main Street*

A great book because it's true.
H. G. WELLS: "One of the greatest novels I have read for a long time. I wish I could have written *Babbitt*." $2.00

### Queen Victoria
(Popular Edition)
*By* LYTTON STRACHEY

A new edition of this famous biography at one-half its original price.
From the plates of the $5.00 edition, $2.50

### Hunters of the Great North
*By* VILHJALMUR STEFANSSON
Author of *The Northward Course of Empire*

For boys — and others who love an account of adventure and exploration in the Arctic regions. Illustrated, $2.50

### Rootabaga Stories
*By* CARL SANDBURG

Fantastic stories for young people of all ages, drawn from the rich soil of American life. "Sublime nonsense — America keeping abreast of Swift and Gulliver." — *N. Y. Times*.
Profusely illustrated, $2.00

### Books and Characters
*By* LYTTON STRACHEY

Lytton Strachey's new book of biography and literary criticism contains fifteen chapters and ranges from 18th Century France to the Victorian age. "Every page is a delight." — *Philadelphia Record*. Illustrated, $3.50

## Rough-Hewn
*By* DOROTHY CANFIELD
Author of *The Brimming Cup*

A story of youth in America and young love in France and Italy. "An unusual and fascinating story that abounds in rich characterization, humorous incident, sentiment and drama." — *The Bookman*. $2.00

### Definitions
*By* HENRY S. CANBY
Editor of *The Literary Review of the N. Y. Evening Post*

A volume of criticism of books and authors, analysis of literary tendencies and studies of significant writers. $2.00

### Modern American Poetry
Edited *by* LOUIS UNTERMEYER
With an historical and critical preface.

### Modern British Poetry
Edited *by* LOUIS UNTERMEYER

From Henley and Stevenson to Masefield, Drinkwater and others who are writing today. (Cloth $2.00 each; the set in limp leather $5.00)

### Continental Stagecraft
*By* KENNETH MACGOWAN *and* ROBERT EDMOND JONES
With 8 Color Plates and 32 Halftone Drawings by Mr. Jones

An account of the most interesting productions of the Continental stages with the new theories of production, scene design and lighting. $5.00

### The Balkan Peninsula
*By* FERDINAND SCHEVILL
Author of *A Political History of Modern Europe*

Professor Schevill's new book is the first in any language to cover the history of the Balkan peoples from the migratory period to the present day. With maps, $5.00

## The Goose Man
*By* JACOB WASSERMANN
Author of *The World's Illusion*

Continental critics consider this Wassermann's greatest novel. It has an immense and colorful background and shows the creative power of this profound student of life. "A world of intolerable beauty." — *N. Y. Tribune*. 477 pages, $2.50

## HARCOURT, BRACE AND COMPANY
1 W. 47TH STREET     NEW YORK CITY

# THE LIVING AGE

VOLUME 315 — NUMBER 4093

DECEMBER 16, 1922

## A WEEK OF THE WORLD

REPARATIONS IN THE FRENCH CHAMBER

PAUL REYNAUD, one of the most brilliant of the younger members of the Chamber of Deputies and an adherent of the National Bloc, delivered a notable speech in the Chamber on October 20, which was listened to with marked attention by a packed house. Although a Nationalist of the same school as President Millerand, he vigorously assailed Poincaré's policy, and ridiculed the Premier's practice of threatening every month or so to seize the Ruhr, and then receding from his bold position and making further concessions to Germany. He compared Poincaré to a threatening dragon breathing forth fire and flame but securely chained to a wall by the tail — a simile that was greeted with vociferous approval by the Deputies.

But the principal points of the speech related to the more fundamental aspeets of the Reparations problem. The speaker argued that Germany was no longer in a position to pay either money or goods upon her Reparations account, a statement that was applauded on the extreme Left and evoked no protest from the Right and the Centre. He also attacked the proposed Stinnes agreement upon political grounds, although he championed an understanding between German and French industrialists. He criticized any policy that tended to amalgamate German and French industries as certain to serve private interests more than they served public interests. This portion of his speech was applauded by the Communists and Socialists and also by the ultra-Royalist reactionary, Léon Daudet, who found himself in rather unusual company on this occasion. The speaker's lucid and matter-oi-fact description of the actual economic condition of Germany was probably the most objective and unbiased statement of this fundamental economic factor in the Reparations question that has been made in the Chamber.

After devoting the first part of his speech to this destructive criticism, Reynaud proceeded to take up constructive measures. His proposal was in substance that France should receive thirty per cent of the capital stock and debentures of all industrial corporations, mining corporations, and similar enterprises in Germany. The proprietors should have the option of redeeming these stocks and debentures with gold whenever they so desired.

This notable address was followed by M. Loucheur's bold and vigorous speech in the Chamber on November 8. The sudden fall of the franc was threatening

*Copyright 1922, by the Living Age Co.*

a political as well as a financial panic. Loucheur is regarded as a man whose political career has not yet reached its zenith. Dr. Rathenau predicted before his death that Loucheur would be master of France within two years. The speaker affirmed that Lloyd George and his British associates at Paris were responsible for the grave error in the original estimate of what Germany could pay.

I remember the tenacity with which Mr. Lloyd George supported the views of his expert. That day it was the sum of 200 milliard gold marks which was fixed as the figure. We think differently to-day. I recalled this to Mr. Lloyd George at Chequers, and he bore me out loyally.

Referring to the Interallied debts, he asserted that America had not lent gold to France, but iron and explosives; the only way to pay her back was in the same materials. 'I do not count the Interallied debts in my calculations. Why? Because we cannot pay them.' This statement elicited great applause.

Turning then to the future policy of France, the speaker declared that the choice was 'either a strong exporting Germany that can pay, or our security. ... Between the two I should not hesitate to choose. I choose security.' He would apply this programme by seizing control of Germany's principal industrial territory, though without political annexation.

I do not want a protectorate nor annexation. I do not want to separate the left bank of the Rhine from the rest of Germany; that would be an economic impossibility. I simply want the Prussian functionaries replaced. I desire simply that Interallied military supervision should stop the creation of military organizations in that country against us. M. Clemenceau proposed, like myself, that an Interallied force, placed under the control of the League of Nations, should occupy the left bank. That would not be hard, for it would not be at the charge of the Reich.

This plan — which seems to imply the coöperation of all the Allies, was received with respect but not with unqualified endorsement by the British press. To be sure, the *Nation and the Athenæum* calls it 'the most courageous and most objective utterance that France has listened to since the war.' Loucheur's taxation scheme 'looked an honest and — for France — a drastic endeavor.'

The guide-points of the speech were (1) the substitution of the ideal of political security for that of a ruinous economic drain on Germany; (2) its declaration that the grand aim was safety by way of European reconstruction, not by way of a separatist French policy; (3) its proposal to release the stranglehold on the Rhine, and to substitute occupation in the name of the League of Nations. These are new and bold ideas, and M. Loucheur is a bold man.

None the less his proposals are viewed with some distrust, even by the Tory *Morning Post*, as verging too close, perhaps, to the Dariac Report policy. That journal says:

M. Loucheur's programme is admirable, but, in the face of such difficulties, is it not a trifle too ambitious? To our mind, the supreme task of statesmanship both in France and Great Britain at the present moment is to seek a common understanding, and thereby to renew the Entente. If agreement were reached, then the two Powers might undertake, as Lord Curzon suggested in his City speech, the consideration of the European problem, step by step and country by country. Before Europe can be saved, France and Great Britain must save one another. And the way of salvation is the way of unity.

Léon Daudet, the Monarchist Deputy, prints an alarmist leader in *L'Action Française* to the effect that the whole speech is a plot to overthrow Poincaré.

Loucheur threw his gauntlet into the ring day before yesterday, amid the applause of his clumsy mamelukes of the Left and the extreme Left, as premature candidate for the premiership. Apparently this was the result of an understanding with Millerand and Millerand's principal financial adviser, M. Finaly, director of the *Banque de Paris et des Pays-Bas.* What is proposed, I repeat, is a petroleum and hydroelectric Cabinet, representing an alliance between the omnipotent American oil magnates and M. Loucheur himself.

✣

A FARMERS INTERNATIONAL

THE movement toward internationalism goes on apace under the pressure of post-war conditions. We hear of International Free Trade Congresses at Budapest and Frankfort-on-the-Main, of the International Labor Conference at Geneva, and now of an International Farmers Conference at Spa, the Belgian health resort made familiar to the whole world as the site of the German headquarters, and of important meetings between the representatives of Germany and the Allies after the war. This congress was called by the farmers, farm managers, and farm laborers of Belgium, and representatives from nine countries were present. Among other resolutions they adopted was: —

Believing it to be the best means of promoting a general accord among nations, that will foster progress, and the well-being of individuals and communities; that will guarantee the rights and interests of the agricultural population, and raise agricultural production to the maximum: —

We declare that we are firmly resolved to cultivate a spirit of peace among nations; to secure the general participation of the farming population in the guidance of international policy, and directly to promote closer relations between governments;

And we resolve to form at once an International Farmers Association, directly representing the desires of the cultivators. . . .

It will be recalled that a 'Green International,' called into life particularly to resist the extension of 'Red Internationalist' encroachments upon the right of private property as applied to peasant holdings, has been agitated, and indeed is reported to be already functioning to some extent in Southeastern Europe.

Mr. Victor Baret, a leading promoter of the Spa Conference, believes that the international spirit that must precede a true reconciliation of nations can be propagated among farmers faster, perhaps, than among any other class.

Assemble the diplomats, the financiers, the captains of industry, from the rest of Europe and the world. You will at once discover that the views and attitudes of the representatives of each country are profoundly different from those of their neighbors. The Germans will view things largely from the point of view of State control and State assistance, in which they have been drilled from infancy. The French and the Belgians will be temperamentally inclined to waive material and immediate interests for sentimental objects; even the Americans, although more realist, will also be moved by a certain idealism. And the English will refuse to consider any subject that is not immediately important and pertinent to the problems of the hour. In a meeting of so many minds, more or less rigidly controlled by past training and prejudices, it is difficult to agree on a common programme, no matter how sincerely each desires to do so. Experience has proved that all too plainly.

But we farmers, no matter whence we come, have the common sympathies inherent in our calling; we have the same cares and the same preoccupations, no matter what our country may be. This gives us a common meeting-ground, irrespective of nationality.

✣

JOFFE AT PEKING

WE published on November 4 an account of the reception of Joffe, the new Soviet envoy at Peking. Eric von Salzmann, the veteran China correspondent of *Vossische Zeitung*, gives a supplementary version of this incident which is not without interest to Western readers. The magnificent embassy buildings of the Tsar's government at Peking are still in the hands of the foreign diplomatic corps and administered by the Dutch Ambassador there. Joffe is living in a private residence rented from a Chinaman.

It is amusing to observe how fanatically the foreign-language press pounced upon Joffe and his mission, even before he opened his mouth. Dr. Joffe said to me personally that he had never had such an experience before, and would not have considered it possible. He was particularly surprised because everyone at Genoa, beginning with Lloyd George himself, had treated him in a friendly and confidential manner. Here in Peking, however, he encounters an almost incredible distrust and reserve. What he remarks most is that the imperialist, capitalist English-language and French-language press of China assume the attitude of running the country and prescribing what the Chinese shall do.

'Tell me,' said Joffe, 'what all these newspapers want of me? Am I really in China? Is this an independent country or a foreign colony? Every little sheet is telling me what to do. My plans and my antecedents are the smallest part of their tale. Every little editor presumes to notify me with what Chinese I must associate and what Chinese I am forbidden to see. They are in a fine fury because I address the University of Peking and its students, who gave me such a cordial reception, and whose President, Tsai, referred to Russia as China's teacher.' . . .

A person familiar with the Far East will experience no surprise. For twenty-two years foreigners have assumed to play the same rôle in this country as the Occupation authorities arrogate to themselves in our Western provinces. Twenty-two years is a long time, almost a generation. They have become so accustomed to that attitude that they cannot conceive anything else.

But it will be different. Joffe is merely playing the overture for a new drama. He vastly overestimates the China press. Public opinion in this country is made in a different way. It pursues invisible channels peculiar to the Orient, of which most foreigners know nothing. Reports of what the Russian ambassador has said circulate with the speed of the wind from tea-house to tea-house, from mouth to mouth. By highway and byway, by railway and riverboat, from the centre to the farthest confines of the Empire, people are saying everywhere: 'Liberty is dawning, and this Russian is its herald.' That is precisely what Joffe intends.

Joffe's message is: 'I want no treaties; I want no concessions; I am here merely to tell you that Russia is alive; I want to show you that Russia is a great member of the family of nations. . . . Russia wants to live in peace with everyone. Russia has no imperialist aims, but she wishes to bring enlightenment to the impoverished masses wherever the victims of imperialist and capitalist exploitation are to be found. They pretend that I am here as a Bolshevist propagandist. I have no such design. If the Chinese ask me to speak to them I shall merely state the facts. If foreigners call that propaganda I cannot help it.'

✢

FASCISTI IN HUNGARY AND BAVARIA

HERR VON RAKOVSKY, Hungarian Minister of the Interior, in a recent address to the voters of his district said: 'The Fascisti movement in Hungary threatens the very existence of the State, for it seeks to undermine and not to strengthen order and discipline in the State.' Commenting upon this, *Pester Lloyd*, a journal of unquestioned bourgeois orthodoxy, says: —

The public knows that an intensely active secret movement is going on to form a Mussolini organization here. . . . But there is a very essential difference between the Italian Fascisti and the men who are imitating their methods and slogans in Hungary. . . . The Italian Fascisti have a Mussolini to lead them, a man who uses revolutionary methods, it is true, but only for the purpose of reëstablishing the shaken authority of the Government, and to fight a form of revolution that would destroy that authority. His whole conduct, since his appointment as Premier, proves that he merely sought to abolish a weak and vacillating rule that feared to take vigorous measures against those who plotted to overthrow the State. . . . But the men who are promoting the Hungarian Fascisti movement are not of this sort, nor do they seek this object. . . . They do not aim to strengthen discipline in the State, but to demoralize that discipline.

Apparently the Government takes this view of the new organization and its aims; for the Home Office has prohibited the Society. Former Premier Stephen Friedrich, the Royalist leader recently under trial as leader of the conspirators who assassinated Tiza, was discovered to be at the head of the movement. The secret pledge of the Hungarian Fascisti included an oath of allegiance to the Hapsburg dynasty; and their confiscated records disclose the fact that their aims were directed against both neighboring States and the present Government. They tried to enlist influential Israelites in their ranks, but at the same time were decidedly anti-Semite. Among their expressed objects was the 'education of the youth of Hungary in the spirit of Attila.'

Meanwhile, several of the largest papers in Southern Germany are displaying suspicious enthusiasm for the Fascisti victory in Italy, and rumor has it that a similar organization is being formed at Munich and perhaps elsewhere in Bavaria. This Bavarian group is led by an Austrian agitator, and is primarily anti-Jewish. It professes not to be monarchist, but presumably has the secret support of the Royalists. Its programme, like the original programme of the Fascisti in Italy, is principally negative — to do away with the parties, politicians, and programmes that have ruled Germany since the revolution. Its professed tactics are direct action; and it repudiates parliamentary methods and majority rule.

NEWS BARRIERS IN EUROPE

ADMIRERS of Pierre Loti will be happy to know that the report of his death, which was the occasion of commemorative articles in the European press, is apparently erroneous. Possibly the mistake was due to confusing him with another Julien Viaud in the French Naval Service.

The fact that a mistaken rumor of this kind should stand uncorrected speaks volumes for the disorganization of European news service since the war. The people are too poor to pay for better news facilities. Not only railway service, but postal and telegraphic communication have suffered to an extent that Americans can scarcely realize. Not since the invention of the telegraph have the countries of central and eastern Europe known less about what goes on in their neighbors' territory than to-day. Not long ago a coal-mine catastrophe occurred in Transylvania, where two hundred and twelve miners were buried alive. Not a word of this reached the press for more than a week, because the news boundary between Rumania and Hungary, which is the usual route by which such a press notice would travel, had become practically impervious to such reports. Vienna used to be the news centre of Austria-Hungary, the Balkans, and the Near East. The *Neue Freie Presse* and other papers of similar standing had their own correspondents and news collectors in every important centre throughout this territory. Now, no paper, especially in a country having a depreciated currency, can afford such facilities. As a result, the circulation of news from one country to another is left mainly to semi-official state-subsidized agencies, which send out nothing unfavorable to their own countries. Even newspapers like the great Berlin dailies, that can afford to employ foreign correspondents, now have to rely mainly on local journalists whose messages are written with an eye to securing the approval of the officials where they reside. An Hungarian journalist who ventured to criticize certain conditions in his own country, in an article in a Vienna newspaper, was recently tried for treason, and condemned to two years' loss of civil rights. In Bavaria, what is practically life-imprisonment has been imposed on newspaper writers for the same offence. The result is that the foreign despatches, even in many of the larger Berlin dailies, consist mainly of gleanings from the press of adjoining countries. This news isolation naturally disposes the people of each country to become more and more wrapped up in their local affairs and prevents good understanding between nations.

A very recent illustration of this condition is given in the following Amsterdam dispatch to the London Times: —

The Telegraaf states this evening that, to its great regret, it will not be able for the present to publish reports and letters about the political situation in Italy from its correspondent in Rome, the Italian Foreign Office having thought fit to inform the Rome correspondent of the Telegraaf that the way in which he is writing about the Fascist movement in Italy, and about the new Fascist régime, does not meet with the approval of the Government now in power.

The letter from the Italian Foreign Office to the correspondent, the text of which has not yet reached the Telegraaf, contains a warning that the correspondent will have to bear the eventual consequences should he maintain his present attitude.

The Telegraaf suggests that these 'consequences' would be expulsion, and it adds that it is not a proof of firmness that a Government should consider it necessary to embark upon such a course of intimidation and direct infringement of the right of free expression of thought. From Signor Mussolini, in particular, who has had a long journalistic career, and should be well aware of the difficulties with which a journalist is confronted, such action was not to be expected.

*

AN UNPUBLISHED CRISPI ANECDOTE

THE article upon Crispi published in the Living Age of November 18 has brought the editor an interesting note from a reader whose family was in the American diplomatic service in France, Italy, and Austria many years ago. During this prolonged sojourn abroad, members of the family became connected by marriage with prominent families in Europe. A daughter by one of these alliances — more French than American by birth and breeding — related, during a visit to this country several years ago, the following incident. During her girlhood, she had made the acquaintance of young Count Crispi, and a tender attachment, ultimately leading to an engagement, had sprung up between them.

He must have been a veritable Don Juan to hold so long the sentimental interest of a woman. Taking out a box of old love letters and many still treasured gifts, among them a cameo pin he had had made for her with his head on it, she said the trouble was all because of their opposing religious beliefs. She, of course, was strongly Roman Catholic. Each thought the other would give in, until the time for the marriage drew near, when she found there was no hope of converting him. So, she said: 'I rose and left the room, and never saw him afterwards.'

# A LEVY ON CAPITAL

[*The proposal to impose a levy upon capital, especially upon fortunes acquired during the war, for the purpose of reducing public debts, is widely mooted in Europe. Switzerland defeated such a proposal by a heavy majority on December 3. The Labor Party in Great Britain advocates the same measure. Many Frenchmen would compel Germany to adopt a similar device to pay her Reparations claims. The affirmative argument which we give below is from the Radical Liberal* New Statesman *of November 11; the negative is from the Moderate Conservative* Spectator *of the same date.*]

I

THERE could hardly be a worse subject than the Capital Levy as the chief issue in a general election. It is even more intricate and technical than tariff reform. Probably it is not exaggerating to say that ninety per cent of the electorate and quite fifty per cent of the politicians are incapable of explaining or understanding either the case for a capital levy or the case against it. Mr. Bonar Law now admits that he was in favor of it in 1917. Circumstances have altered since then, and he is perfectly entitled to say that he has changed his mind. But to go further and denounce it as 'absolute lunacy,' as he did in a recent speech, without giving any substantial arguments against it, is merely throwing dust in the eyes of the electorate. There is still a strong case for it, and there is also a strong case against it.

The strongest argument in its favor is, of course, that the high rate of income tax which existing debt-charges render necessary is a serious handicap to the development of new business by enterprising men of the rising generation. If industry is not to stagnate, it is vital to encourage new men with little or no capital behind them to take risks and seize any new openings for profitable enterprise which may arise. But it is just these men that the continued existence of a huge national debt will most penalize. If there is no levy, they will have to hand over every year, perhaps for the rest of their lives, an annual toll on the fruits of their enterprise for the benefit of holders of war loans, many of whom will have retired from productive work. In other words, while under a capital levy the burden would fall on the present owners of wealth, without it a large contribution will be made by younger men, who are now poor — partly because most of them were called upon to fight during the war instead of staying behind to make money and invest in war loans. This is not merely a sentimental argument; it is sound economic argument as well.

But there is another aspect of the capital levy to which little attention has been paid, either by its advocates or by its opponents. That is the monetary aspect. What effect will the decision, either for or against, have upon the level of prices and the purchasing power of money? Would a capital levy involve inflation or deflation? Would it delay or assist the stabilization of currency and exchanges which is so much needed and is, indeed, by far the most important object which the Government should seek to achieve?

Paradoxically enough, it is sometimes held, even by experienced bankers and business men, that a capital levy would involve inflation. The argument apparently is that since the majority of people assessed would be unable to raise the necessary capital and would find it impossible to realize on stocks and shares when everybody else was trying to do the same, they would have to go to their banks and obtain a bank loan to enable them to pay their contribution. This expansion of bank loans would mean inflation and a general rise in prices.

This argument appears to be radically unsound. In the first place, the number of people who would be unable to find the money at once is not likely to be very great. If the levy was for only half the amount of the national debt, the greater part would be paid off without difficulty by the majority of contributors, by simply handing in war stock to be cancelled. Secondly, the difficulty of realizing on other stocks and shares is exaggerated, since many war-debt holders would be receiving cash from the Government in excess of their individual contribution to the levy. Though the assistance of the banks might be required to tide over an awkward interval, sellers on the Stock Exchange would eventually be met by an equal number of buyers with new cash in their pockets. Lastly, people who were unable to raise money owing to their capital being locked up in their own business would not be compelled to borrow from the bank. If the Government allowed them to pay by instalments at a lower rate of interest than they could borrow from the bank, they would certainly not ask for a bank loan to discharge their liability at once. The view that the levy would mean inflation therefore falls to the ground.

The argument that the levy would involve deflation is far more convincing. Prima facie it is the strongest argument against it. Indeed, in other countries a capital levy has generally been imposed for this object — in Czechoslovakia, for example, where the value of the currency has been greatly improved by this expedient. Government stock is in a sense merely interest-bearing currency. It has largely replaced gold as the backing for notes and deposit liabilities, and Treasury bills in the hands of bankers are only one stage removed from cash, for they can be turned into cash at any time on maturity. Would not a capital levy, by reducing the total volume of Government indebtedness, have the effect of contracting credit, or at any rate contracting the credit-base? To those people who wish to see deflation carried still further, this will be an argument in its favor; but most of us are tired of falling prices and want to see trade recovering. Anything that reduced the credit resources of the country might check recovery.

It is difficult to pronounce with confidence on this issue. But another way of looking at the problem suggests that the levy might actually promote stabilization. According to this argument the danger that lies before us is a movement towards what is called 'secondary' inflation. At the present level of prices we cannot afford to carry the burden of a vast debt incurred at a time when prices were much higher; the national income is not large enough to pay this increased liability for pensions and war debt in addition to other necessary expenditure. If there is no levy, further inflation is almost inevitable. As we have seen, Government debt can be turned into cash either directly by the banks, or indirectly by traders and others, by pledging it as collateral for bank advances. This they will try to do to the fullest extent as soon as trade begins to revive. Have we not here a case for the levy on the ground that it will check an otherwise inevitable drift towards inflation and help to stabilize the existing level of prices?

The underlying issue therefore appears to be this. Can the holders of war loans expect to succeed in maintaining the commodity value of the debt at its present level? Without an enormous increase of production such as took place in America after the Civil War, it is difficult to see how this is possible. Two alternatives are therefore open. Either there will be no levy, in which case prices will rise till the decreased burden of the debt bears a tolerable relation to the national income; or the levy will be imposed, and prices will be stabilized round about their present level. In either case the commodity value of the total national indebtedness will be reduced — in the first case by inflation, in the second by partial cancellation. Since wages always tend to lag behind prices during a period of inflation, it is obvious that the second alternative would be the best for the wage-earning masses. It would also probably be the best for the majority of middle-class taxpayers, and certainly, as we have seen, for the men who fought in the war and are now starting in business.

We do not think that a Labor Government would find it an easy task to carry through its proposal in the face of solid opposition on the part of the banks. But we are by no means sure that the banks themselves may not eventually be driven to recommend it. The banks fought for a long time against the raising of the bank-rate in 1919. They did not like dear money any more than they now welcome the idea of a capital levy. Then, as now, the foremost economists saw a little further ahead and warned them that dear money was a painful necessity. The severity of the slump from which we are now suffering is largely due to the opposition of the City to the only possible means by which the post-war boom could have been prevented from getting out of hand. Dear money is now seen to have been necessary, and most experts agree that it was too long delayed.

Rightly regarded, the capital levy may prove to be the quickest way of stabilizing prices in this country and preparing the way for the restoration of a free gold market. We believe that the banks will sooner or later endorse it as a sound and necessary remedy. It will not be imposed by a Labor Government, for the probability is that a Conservative or Liberal Government will have been forced to adopt it before a Labor Government comes into power.

II

THE Capital Levy is the subject of more confused thinking than any other subject now before the public. That being so, we desire to examine without heat and without prejudice the nature of the proposal and the consequences of its adoption.

We will take the most moderate of the many suggestions made by the Labor Party and not the plans for using the levy to put an end to private property under an 'Instalments System.' That is to say, we will take the case of a capital levy of twenty-five per cent on a man's whole fortune above £5000 — the happy sum which a man may apparently own without either a qualm or a tax, a sum which a cynic has wickedly declared shows that the Chiefs of the Labor Party are 'fairly comfortably off' after all. Let us, as well as we can, trace the exact practical results of the summons to every man over the datum line to surrender a fourth of his total wealth of all kinds. The first thing that would happen would be a universal valuation. The biggest guessing-competition the world has ever seen would be the order of the day, for, remember, valuation is in the last resort only guessing. Nothing but the auction-room ascertains real values, and that often only on a particular day in a particular year.

> The real worth of anything
> Is just as much as it will bring,

and not a sworn valuer's shot at it, however skilful.

And here we may say parenthetically that this is why we have hitherto always taxed income rather than capital. The reason for doing so is a very simple one. Income values itself. Capital does not, and therefore you have to guess at its value. To put it in another way, it is always possible, granted that you can defeat perjury and other forms of dishonesty, to find out what is a man's income, to discover what he has received, or what has been paid to his banking account, within a year. He has got it, or has had it, in his hand, and you can settle his contribution to the State in any way you will. You can ask for a quarter, or a third, or a half, or three quarters of what he has received. The thing is merely a question of law and arithmetic when you are taxing income.

When you tax capital you are in a very different position. You have to make an estimate of, that is make a guess at, the value of a man's property. Whereas income, as we have said, values itself, it requires an army of guessers and counter-guessers to arrive at the money value of capital. The exact amount of income expressed in terms of cash is determinate. The exact amount of capital so expressed is indeterminate.

But this difficulty of knowing what is the value of land which has not been put up to auction or to any kind of sale for the last fifty or sixty years, or, again, of knowing what blood-horses, or pearl necklaces, or Leonardo drawings, or pictures by Memling or Sir Joshua will fetch, is as nothing compared with some of the other difficulties connected with a capital levy. Even if you entertain a blind belief in the capacity of Levison and Golding (late Goldburger), valuers for probate duty, to guess what Mr. Jones's property will fetch at auction at a particular moment, you are by no means out of the woods. If twenty-five per cent of everybody's capital is demanded on the first of January in one year, the vast majority of persons ordered to pay will have to sell stock, or land, or houses, or diamonds, or other valuable non-income-producing possessions, to meet the demand. But now comes in the trouble. Let us take a specific case.

Jones is a capitalist. When the valners have made their valuation, they find that the capital owned by him of all sorts amounts to £100,000. The levy on capital is twenty-five per cent, and therefore he will have to pay £25,000. But Jones has not got this money in bullion or banknotes in his cellar or at the bank, and can produce it only in two ways — either by selling something or by borrowing the money from his banker or from some other person whose function it is to lend money. Now, if Jones were the only man paying a capital tax, or if he were one of a group which numbered only a thirtieth of the capitalists of the country (as in the case of death duties), there would be little trouble about the matter. Jones might feel himself an impoverished man, but he would be able to raise the necessary £25,000, either through his stockbroker or through his banker. But if everybody had got to raise the money at the same moment, Jones would find himself in Queer Street with a vengeance. When he went to his banker for a loan, the banker would say: 'We are very sorry, but the total amount of money we are now in a position to lend is four millions. But by this morning's post we have had applications amounting to four hundred millions. If we lend to you, we should be obliged to ask seventy per cent interest; but that, we admit, is impossible. We can only suggest that you should sell out stock — say, your railway debentures.'

Jones would then repair to his broker, but it would be the same story in different words. The broker would say: 'Unfortunately your debentures, and indeed all stocks, are quite unsalable. The price has dropped to such a point that the best British railway debenture stock can now be purchased to pay eighty per cent, and yet there are practically no buyers, but only sellers. In fact, it is useless for you to think of selling when everybody else is trying to do the same. For our transactions there must be a seller and a buyer, and the buyer is for the moment an extinct mammal.'

What is Jones to do? If he is a man of mental resource, he may possibly go off to the tax collector and say to him: 'I cannot pay you that £25,000 in cash, because I cannot raise it. But I'll tell you what I will do. Here is the sworn valuation that the Government valuer made of my possessions in order to ascertain what I had to pay: that is, the list of capital values which you accepted as the basis on which I was to be taxed. You will see that in the list there is a pearl necklace valued at £2000, and a diamond tiara also at £2000. That makes £4000. My collection of drawings from the Old Masters is put down at £2000, and my Raeburn of the Scots Judge at £6000. That makes £12,000 in all. There is a block of railway debentures down for £8000, and my house in the country is valued at £15,000, which, less the mortgage of £10,000, is £5000. In all, these make £25,000. I propose to hand them over to the Government in lieu of cash. They surely cannot refuse. To do so would be to deny that they are worth the sums which the Government valuer placed upon them only six weeks ago.'

What would be the answer of the capital-tax collector? In spite of Jones's logic, it would, we fear, be a flat refusal to take payment in kind. He would tell the embarrassed capitalist that the State did not want diamonds or houses in the country. It wanted, and must have, money down. To this the capitalist would have to reply: 'Very well, then, come and take it. Perhaps you will be able to arrange a sale. All I know is that I can't.' And very likely he would add: 'Oh, by the way, I got a letter this very morning from the man to whom my country house is mortgaged. He says he must foreclose if he does not have his money out of me by Monday, as he has got to pay his capital levy. Thank Heaven it is you, not I, who'll have to deal with him now you've got Sindercombe. I wish you joy of him. He's a perfect beast!'

No doubt the pure Socialist would, if he were frank, say that all these objections we have raised are nothing to him, that he would be perfectly willing to see the nation paid in kind, and that he would go on taxing capital at the rate of twenty-five per cent per annum till the whole of the capital of the country was taken out of the hands of individuals and lodged in the hands of the State. Those, however, who are not of this extreme kind, and who very possibly are not Socialists though converted to the idea of a capital levy, will probably say that they have a plan which will perfectly well meet all these difficulties. They will, of course, require a valuation of a man's property to ascertain what he is to pay, but they do not mean to force all holders of property to throw their goods upon the market at the same time. If a man likes to sell his stock and pay cash, they will give him a considerable discount for money down. If, on the other hand, he cannot avail himself of this offer, and clearly cannot sell his goods, then they will lend him the money with which to pay his taxes! They will not carry out this Utopian proposal directly, but by promising to lend to the bankers the money which the bankers will lend to the taxpayers for the payment of the capital levy.

'Stick, stick, beat dog! Dog, dog, bite pig!'

Of course, the individual subject of the capital levy must pay the bankers interest on their loan, as the bank must pay the Government.

But then, the plain man may surely ask, 'How will things be any better if this is done on a big scale? The raison d'être of the capital levy as proposed by responsible people is to pay off a large part of the national debt. But what is the use of paying off the national debt with one hand and borrowing money with the other in order to accomplish that transaction?' The answer, we suppose, to this apparent absurdity is that the Government, though they made a loan to the impecunious capitalist, would not only force him to pay a higher rate of interest than that at which the Government now borrow, but would also insist that the loan should be only for a short time and that the interest must always be accompanied by a good percentage of repayment instalment. In other words, the loan would only run for, say, at most twenty years.

Those who think that they are going to get out of the difficulty in this way will find themselves vastly mistaken. They will find that they are simply spreading ruin wide throughout the land. There are literally thousands of private persons and business men who could not possibly pay this new tax for the next twenty years in addition to the present income-tax, super-tax, and death-duties, let alone the plan for a more steeply graduated income-tax which is part of the financial programme to which capital levy belongs. It would destroy them.

The fact is that if the Government-loan scheme is examined, the only possibility will be seen to be a loan for a very long period, with a very small annual payment for sinking fund purposes, and a low rate of interest. But when all this had been worked out, plus the expense of a huge new Government Department with a Capital Levy Minister, we should find that all that would have happened would be an increase of the income-tax under the alias of 'interest on capital levy loan.' If the Labor Party insist that people with over £5000 a year must pay more than they do at present — which is all that a capital levy means if scientifically considered and if it is not intended for confiscation — they had far better do so by the plan we have mentioned above, that is, by an increase of the income-tax. By that method they would get the money without creating a new debt to take the place of the old, and they would not indulge in costly collections.

Depend upon it, this is the worst possible method either of raising money or of dealing with the national debt. If the national debt is to be dealt with, as indeed we think it should be, we feel sure that the best way is on some such lines as those which have been advocated before in these columns. We mean the conversion of the debt, voluntarily, of course, into very long terminable annuities — into a ninety-years' lease instead of a freehold. By doing so we should set a term to our indebtedness, and we should not ruin ourselves by some mock-heroic effort at immediate payment.

After all, the debt is a great fact, and we shall not alter that fact by changing its name. Let us assume you take more money than now from the individual in order to pay off debt, and then follow the transaction out in the concrete. You will soon see that you are not creating or saving extra wealth, but only altering its ownership. The individual sells out railway stock in order to pay a Government demand for reducing the national debt. He next receives a portion of the sum — a certain amount will have been used up in the bureaucratic machine — as compensation for the cancellation of twenty-five per cent of such government stocks as he holds. With this somewhat shrunken money he then goes back into the market and buys some more railway stock. Who on earth is going to be the better for this process?

Granted we are not going to repudiate, which we certainly are not, it is better to leave the national debt as it is than to indulge in any of these fantastic schemes. We shall not fall into the paradox of pretending that the national debt is an economic advantage. It is, of course, a very unpleasant record of a loss. But it has one moral or political advantage. So long as the national debt remains as it is, it will prevent any Government from borrowing more, and the less Governments borrow, whether in war or peace, the better.

# LATIN AMERICAN REVOLUTIONS

## BY MANUEL UGARTE

From *La Revue Mondiale*, November 1
(CURRENT AFFAIRS SEMIMONTHLY)

ALL nations have suffered violent shocks when an inevitable transformation has been repressed by their governments until only violence could achieve it. The confined forces ultimately rent asunder their restraining bonds. In this sense the emancipation of the Spanish colonies in América, a little more than one hundred years ago, was an inevitable consequence of their economic, political and social evolution, which had outgrown the administrative system and form of government Spain imposed upon them. Deep-lying causes had prepared the ground for the wars of liberation, and these must be interpreted in history as due to a spontaneous and necessary instinct of the people, and not to mere popular caprice, or to the ambition of individual leaders.

Unhappily, however, we cannot thus characterize the thousands of revolutions, revolts, political overturns, seditions, and *pronunciamientos* since 1810; these have been mostly illogical and causeless, paralyzing the progress of the continent, and discrediting its peoples and its governments. Therefore it is well worth while to consider seriously what has produced this state of chronic revolution and endemic anarchy in countries exceptionally favored by nature, whose inhabitants are able to live comfortably with a minimum of effort.

Possibly this very ease of existence, which has prevented the people from feeling the imperious need of labor, has contributed to dissipate their creative energies, and to make them love doubtful adventures. But we must seek deeper causes for this predisposition to unrest, first of all in the ethnic composition of our people. I do not mean to intimate that our racial mixtures are a fatal and final handicap. We know that when we average its history through the centuries, no nation is constantly and absolutely inferior or superior. The Greeks, the Romans, and the Spaniards of to-day are far from possessing the influence and prestige that they enjoyed at certain epochs of history. On the other hand, many peoples have lifted themselves from a humble place in the world to the rank of conquering and ruling Powers. Countries that have been defeated and reduced to servitude have regained their greatness, and countries that have held sway over broad dominions have sunk into decay and powerlessness. When Cæsar conquered the Gauls he did not dream that Napoleon would one day conquer Italy.

This instability in the relative rank of nations and races justifies our regarding the present condition of Latin America, like that of India, China, Ireland, and certain colonial countries, as not necessarily permanent and possibly to be reversed either by the caprice of fate, or by our own ambition, sacrifice and service to humanity.

When we review Latin America's past, we find two burdens of atavistic anarchy weighing upon her, one derived from her Indian blood, the other from her Spanish blood. It is a common error to imagine that the aboriginal inhabitants of America formed a homogeneous community. When the New World was discovered, it was occupied by a great number of distinct tribes and peoples, who either knew nothing of each other, or hated and fought each other. Some tribes, on account of their larger numbers, their greater progress, or their bravery, ruled over other subject tribes. The normal relations of these peoples were far from harmonious. Except for two great agglomerations, the Aztec and the Inca empire, both of which consisted of many subject peoples ruled by a small dominant tribe or caste, the Indians lived in constant enmity with each other, and their feuds and their tribal wars constituted the whole record of their primitive history. This explains why a few thousand Spaniards were able to conquer millions of men and vast empires. Pizarro and Hernando Cortes were not only bold and able captains, but also shrewd politicians. They won their conquests by turning to their own account the hatreds, the thirst for vengeance, the rivalries, the ambitions of the natives; by sowing the seed of antagonism and distrust among them; and by recruiting from the ranks of weaker tribes allies with whom they overthrew the stronger.

But this victory, won with the weapons of anarchy, did not destroy anarchy, which in time turned against the victors. The Indians who had subdued America for the Spanish conquerors revolted against their successors and formed the rank and file of the revolutionary armies that overthrew their power.

Upon this native stem of mutual enmity and perpetual warfare were grafted the haughty individualism and arrogant jealousies of the newcomers. When we review the history of the discovery of America and the three centuries of Spanish rule that followed, we are astounded at the frequency with which Spanish captains turned aside in the midst of their most heroic exploits to fight each other, and subordinates revolted against commanders. Private feuds and civil wars raged so constantly among the commanders of Spain's conquering expeditions, they formed such an integral part of the deeds of valor and the victories of that period, that we are forced to ask whether the rude personal independence of the conquistadores, their indomitable individualism, was not the secret of their triumph. And after a settled colonial government had been established, the same spirit of haughty self-assertion, the savage insistence upon authority, promoted the interminable disputes among the military, civilian and religious representatives of Spain in America, which obliged the mother-country to send to her new possessions frequent emissaries, whose decisions, given in the name of the King, were not always obeyed. The qualities that aided the Conquest, when every private soldier imagined himself a captain, and every captain imagined himself a sovereign, prepared the way for the faults and feebleness of the colonial government, and degenerated in the young republics that followed, into unceasing conspiracies and dictatorships.

Our Latin American revolutions are not mere accidents. Even if we disregard the historical antecedents I have just mentioned, they obey well-defined general laws; for we discover that these revolutions pursue the same course and have the same features in countries remote from each other, and they have gradually disappeared in certain zones where the conditions that promoted them have ceased to exist.

Among the indigenous causes of revolution in Latin America were first of all the disappointment of the natives over the failure of independence to benefit them personally. Liberation from Spain proved to be but a change of masters. The new republics were governed by an élite consisting mainly of the descendants of Europeans; and the old Spanish social and economic régime, which took no account of the interests of the natives, continued unchanged. So the Indians, finding themselves excluded from the new government, formed a restive population that political adventurers easily played upon for private ends.

The result was a constant series of revolutions which, however, were further encouraged by other favoring circumstances. Chief among these was the subdivision of the old Spanish Empire in America into a host of petty States whose capricious frontiers, small population, and lack of organic national unity and vigor, made them the easy prey of bold adventurers. Possessing no regular armies to speak of, and governed by men of little experience in the art of administration, they were the ready victims of violence and surprise. Often a mere handful of rebels was able to overturn a government insecurely seated in power and unsupported by national precedents and traditions.

The second condition that encouraged revolution was the illegal status of many existing governments, whose authority was derived from an armed revolt or an electoral farce. Such a government naturally had no moral weight behind it. The very example of its success encouraged others to employ identical means to usurp its authority.

A third important factor in Latin America's political instability remains even today—the absence of commercial and industrial interests, powerful enough to insist upon social equilibrium and an orderly political régime.

Undoubtedly in every Latin American country, even in those where discord is the most chronic, a majority of the people disapprove of violence and desire an end to profitless agitation. This majority belongs to two groups: a very numerous class who simply ask for personal security and to be left alone, and an influential upper class, intelligent enough to understand the evils of political anarchy and the injury it does the country. We must explain the inactivity, the silence, the submissiveness of this majority of peace-loving or enlightened citizens by the fact that the social and political institutions amid which they live are still in process of formation, and this is a stage of development where vices are apt to be more self-assertive than virtues.

In those South American republics where economic progress has now made considerable headway, where the laboring and thinking classes feel that they have at last got the better of the conspiring and adventuring elements, where a real national organization has been achieved, where elections are conducted according to law, it is becoming either difficult or impossible to start revolutions. As the people have become better educated and prosperity has increased, the view of the masses has broadened and professional agitators are compelled to pursue their objects according to the rules of democratic government.

However, the old spirit of rivalry and intrigue still survives in the relations between neighboring countries. There are no rational conflicts of interest, no long-standing historical traditions — except in one or two special cases — to justify this mutual hostility. None the less we see certain governments that are still quite unable to utilize even a fraction of the natural resources they already possess, inviting fratricidal strife to secure possession of border zones, sometimes of little value, at the expense of neighbors whose social institutions, language and traditions are the same as their own. They are ready to pour out their energy and their wealth to secure a trifling frontier advantage, just as the disordered and revolutionary republics we have described spent their energy and wealth in futile rivalries for the presidency.

So Latin America, whose history and whose interests should ensure her unity, who is exposed, like all feeble peoples possessing vast natural wealth, to the covetousness and ambition of stronger nations, has seen her progress constantly checked by domestic feuds either within the confines of each country, or between the republics that together form her larger whole. This has been highly prejudicial to the interests of her people, whose resources are fast falling into the hands of powerful foreign companies, and whose freedom of action in international affairs is subject to influences that hamper or threaten autonomous action.

These local hatreds are so bitter and relentless, that in Central America foreign aid has been solicited against an enemy clan at home, or a neighboring country of the same blood.

The imperialist nations, following tactics as ancient as they are familiar, seize upon such conditions as I have described, to increase their power and promote their material interests. I shall not discuss the moral justification of such conduct in this purely objective study of historical phenomena. But the fact remains that the imperialist Powers have systematically promoted these disorders for the past hundred years, overthrowing governments that were hostile to them and putting in authority men who were subservient to themselves. They did this in the guise of natural allies and guardians of peace. Revolutionists have received financial support, war materials, and even direct military aid when there was something to gain by giving such assistance. At the same time diplomats have encouraged international friction, so that a powerful outside government might play the part of arbiter. Such proceedings have created unrest and distrust among the common people, who have not known what course to take, and have prevented unity and coöperation among ourselves. Continual revolutions, that instead of serving the cause of liberty to which they appeal merely serve to set up dictatorships, have become a favorite device for ruling alien peoples and controlling their domestic matters. This explains the succession of chaotic events that made Nicaragua, Santo Domingo and Haiti surrender control of their own revenues and accept the protectorate of a foreign power. The same devices separated Panama from Colombia, and are now employed to accomplish the still more difficult task of weakening Mexico.

Some have tried to explain the constant agitation of Latin America by arguing that her republics are young and must sow their wild oats before they arrive at wisdom and maturity. But this theory is disproved by the example of the United States, also a young nation. That country's domestic peace has been broken but once, and then over the irreconcilable issue of slavery. This theory is also refuted by the sound and peaceful development of some South American republics, that for many years have avoided revolutionary disturbances. A signal illustration of this was the recent election of Señor Alvear as President of Argentina, at a time when he was absent from the country.

Therefore we must conclude that the evil is not a necessary one, but a curable disease, that can be relieved or healed by appealing to an ideal — the preservation of the fatherland; and by two physical remedies — railways and schools.

Men may be right in attributing our Spanish American revolutions to inexperience; but that inexperience is not due to youth, but to lack of knowledge; and that is perhaps a more hopeful explanation, for nations cannot grow old at will, but they can always educate themselves.

We are not assuming too much in predicting that the evolution of our Spanish American republics, hampered as it has been by difficulties at home and by intervention from without, is approaching a stage where our political leaders will cease to be preoccupied mainly with party rivalries and with empty controversies with neighboring countries, and will envisage in its full amplitude the broader problem of living together in harmony, and of doing the things that favor, and avoiding the things that hamper, the expansion of Latin civilization in the Western Hemisphere.

The great problem of Spanish America is not to discover the particular parties that are best qualified to govern us in an environment without traditions, where men rise easily from one rank to another. Far less is our problem to contest with our neighbors the possession of territories and natural resources, before we have begun even to scratch the wealth in our undisputed patrimony. All the parties that are struggling for political power either have the same platform or no platform at all. Every one of our Spanish American republics can support a population twenty times as dense as at present. Domestic politics and frontier controversies are comparatively unimportant questions compared with the task of raising our economic standards and guaranteeing the development of our present resources by our own people, instead of by powerful foreign corporations. At home our task is to improve the state of our public finances and to organize our production. Abroad our task is to adopt a consistent and coherent policy, seeking particularly a closer alliance with the Latin countries of Europe. In these two directions lie our future safety.

Some Spanish Americans, while recognizing the logic of this programme, object that first of all we must get rid of our present dictators. It cannot be denied that in some Spanish American republics the personal pride and the mutual distrust of political rivals still perpetuate almost impossible conditions. But here a dictum of the French revolution suggests itself: 'Tyranny does not exist because there are tyrants; tyrants exist because there is tyranny.' So long as the atmosphere of revolution and dictatorship remains, one dictator will be overthrown merely to give place to another. Of course the arbitrary governments that still survive in some parts of Latin America are an obstacle to good relations with their neighbors. We must look to the economic and political evolution of the future to remove this blight from our more backward peoples. Popular government is most powerful when it is most pacific. I do not anticipate that our revolutions will cease all at once. Before they finally disappear there may be periods of renewed reaction and disorder. But there are encouraging symptoms. Our younger generation is gradually learning to form living, organic political parties. European immigration is bringing to the New World the idea that politics need not involve force. The common people who have furnished the fuel for these conflagrations are learning wisdom. The partisan leaders — *caudillos* — who have in the past instigated our political disorders, are beginning to be out of date in a society increasingly conversant with cosmopolitan civilization and ideals.

We may look forward to a similar gradual dying out of discord between the republics themselves. Our continent will always be divided into two great camps, distinct in race, language, and civilization. In the same way that every malady ends either in recovery or death, our political malady will end either with a vigorous vital reaction of our own people against these evils, or with our national decadence and eventual subjugation by a foreign power. Labor, unity, peace, are the only defence of the weak. The Latin republics will survive only if they obey the laws of national health; if they become their own healers, and if they seek in Europe, particularly in France, Spain and Italy, an economic, intellectual and moral counterpoise, to guarantee their future and to resist the undue pressure of influences from which they never can entirely escape.

# FROM DUBLIN TO KERRY

## BY E. S. G.

From the *Nation and the Athenæum,* November 11
(LONDON LIBERAL WEEKLY)

FROM Dublin as far as Limerick Junction our journey, if not signalized by an undue haste, was, on the other hand, devoid of unusual incident. Arriving an hour and a half late, we dallied for another hour in the station, while the officials made up their minds whether they would proceed any further or not.

Ultimately, after changing into another train, we set off at a crawl for Buttevant over temporarily restored bridges and railway lines, which are torn up in the night, relaid every few days, only to be torn up again on the following night; the damage perpetrated by the Republicans being encouraged, if not actually inspired, by enterprising car-drivers who are making colossal fortunes conveying passengers and their luggage from one station to the next, and who at Buttevant were waiting in massed formation to fall upon us. The train being unable to proceed further owing to the destruction of a bridge, we had no choice but to transfer ourselves to a jaunting car, and to drive the seven miles to Mallow behind a decrepit horse, in a drenching mist.

At no time a hive of activity, Mallow —the junction connecting all the lines in the south of Ireland—presents to-day a lamentable spectacle of decay. The magnificent ten-arch bridge across the Blackwater has been blown to pieces, a work of malign ingenuity ascribed to Erskine Childers, assisted by an engineer from Krupps'.

The dingy hotel where we spent the dismal night is situated in the main street of the town amidst the crumbling ruins of such civilization as remained after last year's burning by the Black-and-Tans, followed by the bombs and bullets of the Free Staters and Republicans, whose favorite battle-ground it seems to have been ever since. The windows of the coffee-room were riddled with bullet holes; the floor was carpeted in crumbs; two commercial travelers, with pained expressions on their faces, sprawled in profound slumber over the only two armchairs in the room; on an ink-stained writing table a *Strand Magazine* of 1899 served as literary link between Mallow and the outer world.

After a night of indescribable discomfort, the next morning dawned, if anything, somewhat wetter than the preceding day. After breakfast we started in a hired motor, the driver of which, we were given in confidence to understand, was an Ulster man who had deserted from the British Army, been discharged from the Republican, and was about to offer his services to the Free State — a military record which inspired us with complete confidence in the resourcefulness of his character. Avoiding the main roads, which for several weeks have been completely blocked, we arrived by a circuitous route over a mountain at Millstreet, where our inquiries for the road to Killarney were met with derisive shrieks.

'If you can lepp and you can swim you may perhaps get there; not otherwise,' we were told. 'Every bridge is down and every road is blocked since the fighting on Sunday.'

Conscious of proficiency in both 'lepping' and swimming, we pushed undaunted on our way, running almost immediately into a flying column of Free State troops, who stopped us and demanded the driver's permit. They were covered with mud, weary and war worn, having been fighting for two days.

'You will meet Irregulars further on,' said the officer. 'As you are only ladies they may not take your car; if you had men with you they would certainly do so.'

Bidding him good-bye, we charged with thrilled expectancy into the war zone, an old man who subsequently directed us adding to our growing excitement by informing us that the 'Free *Starters*' had 'gone back' and that the ' '*Publicans*' were on ahead.

Whether the latter were engaged in burying their dead — the number of which, according to the Free Staters, was almost past all calculation — or whether we drove through them, concealed behind the hedges, we never discovered. The disappointing fact remained; we never saw even one member of the phantom army in whose track we were supposed to be following.

'Are you all mad here?' I inquired of a group of men we next came upon, contemplating a gaping void in the middle of a village street, in front of which the car suddenly pulled up — only just in time to prevent our taking a wild leap into the river swirling in the precipitous depths beneath.

'More than half of us,' was the cheerful reply, as a couple (presumably of the sane section) advanced with advice and directions to the driver, whom they conducted down a muddy declivity leading to the river, into which the car plunged — while we crawled, clinging to the parapet, over a narrow footway on to the other side.

When nearly across, the engine of the car — which had been gradually getting into deeper water — suddenly stopped. Our hearts sank. Complete silence fell on the spectators for a moment; after which the entire population of the village, sane and insane, rushed to the rescue, throwing down stones and eventually hauling the car into shallower water where the engine was restarted.

Having regained the road, we next found ourselves up against a gigantic tree, prostrate across our path, its branches sawn in such a fashion as to form snags, — between and underneath which it did not seem possible for any vehicle to pass. But our motor-driver came up to our expectations in the matter of ingenuity, and by lowering the wind-screen and keeping his head to the level of the steering-wheel, advancing and reversing every few inches, the car emerged triumphantly, after a good quarter of an hour's manœuvring, on the other side.

It was the first of many similar obstructions, some of which we struggled under, some of which we squeezed our way round, and others which we avoided altogether by turning in at the gates of private demesnes and bumping our way through farmyards, the walls of which had been pulled down by cars preceding us: experiences so unnerving that at Killarney the driver dumped our luggage down in the middle of the street and bade us a polite but firm farewell.

At the local garages all requests for a car to continue our journey in proved useless. Only by æroplane, we were told, could anybody hope to arrive at Killorglin; 'every bridge is down, and over a hundred trees and all the telegraph posts and the wires twisted in and about and around them.'

After over an hour spent in frantic appeals, the owner of a horse and car was finally prevailed upon to undertake the eighteen-mile drive in consideration for a sum exceeding the first-class railway fare to Dublin.

For the first few miles we made our way through Lord Kenmare's demesne, over the grass, down on the shore of the lake, where the horse had to be led between the rocks and where the wheels of the car sank deep into the sand and gravel. After being almost bogged in a *bohereen* leading into another demesne, which we drove through, we proceeded for about a mile on a side road, when we encountered a broken bridge. A precipitous descent into a wood, across the river, over a field into a lane, on for a mile or two over trenches, getting off the car every five minutes, occasionally having to take the horse out and drag it over felled trees and down into ditches; and then the most formidable river we had yet met, with an insurmountable bank on the opposite shore, topped with a barbed-wire fence. Seeing no possibility of manœuvring this, we drove to a cottage, where a young woman came out and directed us.

'Drive down the bank by the bridge and go under the farthest arch, and then drive down in the river for a bit till you come to a slope in the bank, and you'll see a way up on the other side.'

An old man came out of the cottage and offered to come with us. I walked with him, while the horse and the car started down the river. We talked the usual platitudes, when suddenly, seizing me by the arm, he exclaimed: 'Oh, God! Are n't the times terrible?'

'Indeed they are,' I replied fervently.

He broke into sobs. 'Oh, God!' he cried, 'Oh, God! my only son, he's on the run, and if they get him they'll shoot him. . . . I can't shtop talking of it. . . . That young girl you saw just now, she's my daughter. She's come all the way from England to mind me, but sure, nobody can mind me now. . . . I can't shtop talking, and to-morrow they're taking me to the asylum. . . .'

Looking back, after I had bidden him good-bye and climbed among the broken masonry up the cliff-like side of the tumbled arch, I could see him, still standing by the lonely shore; his rugged, beautiful face distraught with anguish, his hands clasped in mental torture: 'Oh, God! oh, God!' echoing in my ears as we drove on in the fading twilight on the deserted road, his tragic figure leaving in one's memory an unforgettable impression of Ireland's madness and despair.

It was dark when finally we arrived at our destination, having taken five hours to accomplish the last eighteen miles. When it is realized that not a single obstruction we encountered after leaving Mallow would have presented the slightest difficulty to a lorryful of soldiers, armed with a few planks and a couple of saws, the imbecility of the tactics of the Irregulars, which merely cause delay and inconvenience to civilians, can hardly be understood. Yet for months past, bands of able-bodied youths have been engaged in destroying bridges and blocking roads all over the South with no other result. As soon as one road is cleared by the Free Staters another is being obstructed, a work of devastation which will, presumably, only cease when every tree in the country has been felled and every bridge laid low.

Meanwhile, we are a philosophical and long-suffering race, and if on my journey I endured untold fatigue and discomfort, on the other hand I have added considerably to my knowledge of the geography of my native land.

# BULGARIA'S LABOR ARMY

## BY NINO SALVANESCHI

*From La Tribuna, October 26*
(ROME LIBERAL DAILY)

I HAVE been watching a group of 'conscripted workers' laboring on the railway between Sofia and Rovstchovk. They were working away diligently and cheerfully, some twenty men under a foreman. A little farther along was another gang of twenty, and in the remoter distance still another group of the same number. And thus it is the whole length of the line. Men are repairing the roadbed, bridges, and the neighboring highways. They all wear khaki uniforms and bicycle caps.

I have driven about the country here, in the Danube lowlands surrounding Rovstchovk, and everywhere I have watched little groups of twenty or twenty-five men, belonging to Bulgaria's labor army, working in the fields. They, too, work diligently and cheerfully and are in uniform.

All over the country the same thing may be seen. Companies, regiments and divisions of a new labor army, planned and organized two years ago by Stambuliski, are working patiently and persistently to rebuild a new Bulgaria.

England has saved herself financially with her income tax. Bulgaria is saving herself financially with her labor army. Her regular army has been abolished, reduced to a mere police force and frontier guard. In addition, it still supplies the people with the military concerts that they must have at any cost. Indeed the Bulgarian music is excellent, and throngs of people assemble in the parks and public squares whenever a regimental band is announced to play. Gypsy music, formerly so popular, has been largely replaced by Russian balalaika companies.

It is not easy to form an entirely dependable opinion of Bulgaria's system of obligatory labor. The Rumanians and Serbs call it 'forced labor.' The Bulgarians, who are unquestionably the most hard-headed and taciturn of the Balkan peoples, never talk freely about their own affairs. And they say less regarding this institution than any other. When the Supreme Council of Versailles tried to suppress the labor army, because it suspected Bulgaria's real motive was to use it as a substitute for compulsory military service, the Bulgarians published a few documents and two or three pamphlets on the subject. Their argument was that this was the only way that Bulgaria could get back on her feet economically, and restore the value of her currency. Thereupon Versailles left her to do as she pleased.

This was a wise decision. Had the Allies interfered they would have destroyed the best example of coöperative labor organized for social objects, since the war. Little, defeated Bulgaria is being salvaged from the wreckage of ten years of almost constant fighting, by a peasant Government; and her people have put their shoulder to the wheel in a way that might well be envied by the rest of Europe.

The obligatory-labor law was enacted on June 5, 1920, and went into effect twelve days later. Like every radical statute, such an act, limiting the liberty of the individual and compelling every citizen, no matter what his social rank, to engage in manual labor for the benefit of the State, was naturally vigorously resisted by political opponents of the party in power.

So the old army has been abolished and a volunteer national guard maintains order at home, and watches the frontiers. The real Bulgarian army has substituted the spade and the pickaxe for the rifle and the bayonet.

Every man and woman is liable to obligatory labor. Compulsory service for women has not yet been worked out in final form, but it will go into full effect in 1923. Women will be liable to labor duty from their sixteenth to their fortieth year of age.

The period of service for men begins at twenty and continues to their fiftieth year. During the first year they must work for the State for eight months, during which time they are fed, clothed and lodged, but receive no wages. The system of recruiting is regional, the men being enlisted and performing their service in the districts where they reside. These workers are divided into groups of twenty or twenty-five men, and assigned to such employments as: road-building, bridge-building, railway-building, harbor works, factory labor, stone-quarrying, timber-cutting, draining and dyking swamp- and flood-lands, fishing, taking care of animals, and similar services. Naturally since three fourths of the five million people in Bulgaria are peasants, actually engaged in tilling the soil, the primary object of the law is to develop the agricultural resources of the country. Prime Minister Stambuliski says: 'We shall hand over the garden of Bulgaria to our children better cultivated.' Therefore some three fourths of the labor army are detailed to farm work.

And I must say that though Bulgaria was always an excellently tilled country, the effect of this application of intensive coöperative labor under scientific and skilled direction is already producing notable results.

In addition to the eight months of compulsory labor which every man must perform during his twentieth year, he is further liable to twenty days of compulsory labor annually up to his fiftieth year. These twenty days of work are divided into ten days for the profit of the Central Government, and ten days for the profit of the township. After a man has once performed his eight-months service he can commute by a fixed payment in cash the subsequent twenty-days obligatory annual service. The cost of commuting varies from three hundred to seven hundred '*leve*'. However, the proportion of commutations cannot exceed forty per cent of the labor recruits of Sofia, and thirty per cent in the country districts.

The reason for permitting commutation is twofold. Some men, on account of their age, health, or profession, are of very little value as manual laborers in the class of work that the Government can furnish. In the second place, the fees paid for commutation are used by the Government for clothing and feeding other laborers. In fact, these commutation fees will practically pay the whole cost of maintaining the Government's labor force during the year 1922.

The number of first-year service men, who cannot commute their labor by paying a fee, is about thirty thousand. In addition, there are a great number of twenty-day workers who do not commute their service. An appropriation of eighty-six million leve was made for organizing and maintaining the army during the past season. However, only forty-nine million leve of this sum were actually expended. The value of the labor performed is estimated at seventy-five million leve, so a net profit for the State has resulted.

The organization of the compulsory-labor groups does not follow military precedents, except that the men are in uniform, they are fed a standard ration, and they are subject to strict discipline. However, discipline is not much of a problem, for the Bulgarians possess the needed quality by nature. Each twenty or twenty-five workers, as I have said, form a 'group'; five 'groups' form a 'century'; for every three 'centuries' there is a *urednik*, or general superintendent, who in turn reports to a higher official.

No person, no matter what his rank and wealth, is excused from the eight months compulsory service. The older laborers are assigned, for the ten days they must work for the Central Government, to the service of different Ministries — agriculture, war, commerce, public works, and railways.

When the law is applied to women it is proposed to organize two categories — country workers and city workers. Their periods of service will be considerably shorter than those of the men, probably three months. Part of their duty will be to make the uniforms and do the laundry work of the male labor army. During their period of service the younger girls — those sixteen years old — will be given practical training in domestic economy.

## AIR TRAVEL IN RUSSIA

### BY GEORG POPOFF

From the *Frankfurter Zeitung*, November 5
(LIBERAL DAILY)

'EIGHT hours by airplane from Konigsberg to Moscow!' A morning with the Prussians and an evening with the Russians. That sounds worth while. Besides, it enables the traveler to dispense with a Lett visa, with a teapot, with private bed-linen and with all the formalities required of a traveler on the Russian railways. It is not necessary to shake *Tovarish Provodnik* out of his sound slumber to get hot water. Last of all, the eternal question of food is reduced to a minimum. In eight hours you are in Moscow. Could anything be more convenient!

Our sleeping-car from Berlin brought me to Konigsberg just when its citizens were awakening from their morning slumber. There was a light mist, and frost. While waiting for the morning fog to clear, so that we could start on our journey, I contemplated with amazement the great stack of courier sacks that we were to carry with us — hundreds of kilos.

'Have those got to go?'
'Yes, certainly.'

The next question is: Who is the pilot to-day? A Ukrainian name is given. So, a Russian pilot. During the war the Russians developed some splendid aviators. But passenger flying is really a German development. I was about to make an observation to that effect when the propeller began to hum and further words were as vain as they were superfluous. A minute later I was half boosted, and half pulled myself, into the comfortable coupé of the flying vehicle. Three crosses! Kismet! Good-bye, Germany!

Starting is supposed to be the most dangerous part of the trip. I did not know that yet. For that reason I studied with unconcerned gratification the little city beneath us while I held a flask of cognac in my hand. Our Russian courier, Comrade Schulman, was hastily buckling up a thick, sealed package — Litvinov's report to Lenin on the Urquhart agreement — secrets with seven seals. The machinist, who sat also in the cabin, *Tovarish* Soldatkin, shouted in my ear that Rolls-Royce motors are much better than all our German motors taken together. I nodded silently and unprotestingly.

Hosts of new impressions were crowding their way into my consciousness. There, below us, was a long stretch of gardens. At first beautifully kept grounds with flower-beds and fountains, surrounding pretty villas. These soon made way for tiny square checkers of land — a tract of workingmen's allotments. These social distinctions became remarkably clear, when one absorbed them from a sufficiently lofty vantage point. You can learn a great deal in the air.

At Kovno, which we reached in less than an hour and a half, our airplane was scheduled to stop for only half an hour, for the purpose of replenishing oil and fuel. But our luggage must be examined. And if — horrible thought! — your Lithuanian visa is not in order, you are likely to have abundant leisure to ponder on Border State problems and any other questions that may chance to interest you, in the casemates of Kaunas. I am a man who respects the laws of every country, and therefore prided myself on the possession of an uncriticizable Lithuanian visa.

*Tovarish* Soldatkin's official stamp, however, was one day out of date. No one knew what to do: imprisonment for life or immediate execution? There was a long whispering conversation — perhaps some money passed from hand to hand. Two hours were lost. Great clouds began to chase across the heaven toward Moscow. We did not move. At last the sky cleared. Soldatkin's visa was extended. The propeller hummed merrily, sunshine flooded our hearts, and no one thought of coming dangers.

The airplane was again in motion. For a few seconds only I was conscious that our wheels still struck the earth at intervals. Then we were up and away. A minute later — and there was a shattering detonation. The airplane kept on its way, but a glance at the horrified and chalk-white face of Soldatkin told me that something dreadful was happening. Another and a louder explosion followed. There was no time for thinking. An invisible power seemed to hurl us with a Titanic angry gesture toward the ground. Just a moment of chilling terror, and then hopeless, passive resignation to inevitable death. No one knew just what followed. The airplane drove headlong toward earth, and capsized like lightning. In spite of that, the crashing of the walls and window panes and propeller lasted for several seconds as the plane settled down upon unbelievably heavy objects — trunks, er bags, and other articles, violently against our backs. Our only thought was: 'Then there was a sudden silence. Perhaps it lasted or two, while we w Some one groaned. suffocating odor sur gasoline was flowing ments of the moto thought occurred and burn us up.

from under the mass that was crushing us. Hands and feet held fast. Pieces of glass cutting into our flesh.

I suddenly heard some one running about excitedly over the shattered wings. It was *Tovarish* Soldatkin, the first to extricate himself.

'The devil! Lift that accursed courier bag from my back. Quicker, or I'll suffocate.' And good Soldatkin did his best. All three of us needed his help. Finally, I was liberated. The pilot with the Ukrainian name hung head-downward, his legs entangled with the steering-gear; his face was one mass of blood. Still, it was Comrade Schulman, the courier, who was injured worst. Fractured skull, it turned out later. His face was perfectly yellow; he was in a stupor, like a man in a trance, and did not speak a word. He was later taken to the hospital. The airplane was a tangled wreck. Just ahead of the place where we struck was an excavation twenty-five feet deep. Had we gone a few steps further on, not a man would have been left alive. When I saw this, I drew a little comfort from it. Then I took some pictures of what remained of our airplane. It was an unrecognizable mass of fragments. By this time a crowd came up to our assistance. You can imagine how we escaped.

does not sound so bad. What is a lit? It is the new currency introduced yesterday, October 1. Misfortunes never come singly. Ten lits — the first syllable of 'Lithuania' — are equal to one dollar. So twenty lits is two dollars. At the present rate of exchange this means 4000 marks! A pretty expensive room, but a fine kind of money. Some one suggested: 'How would it be if we folks in Germany introduced a *deut?*' However, we are in no mood for joking. We want to sleep, sleep, and sleep, and to forget the currency, the Border States, airplanes, couriers, Urquhart, and all the rest.

The next day Moscow was still as far away as ever. We could not fly because it was cloudy, and there were other obstacles in the way. 'But tomorrow you'll surely reach Moscow.' So there's nothing to do but wait. However, the eternal food question kept presenting itself. The Government hotel has a Government restaurant. The menu card is printed in Lithuanian and French, although most of the people here speak only German or Russian. However, Germans have not much difficulty with a Lithuanian menu card. I quote verbatim from the one at this hotel: *Snellklopsas, Roastbeefs, Snitzelas, Zwiebelklopsas.*

Our third morning from Konigsberg. A German pilot was on hand. The propellers began to roar; we flew on, naturally in another airplane. Comrade Schulman, who was left behind seriously injured, was replaced by Comrade Soldatkin. It was he who now held the package with seven seals, grasped tightly in his hands. Let's hope it did not reach Moscow too late. While we were testing the toughness of modern airplanes and of our own ribs, and taking lessons in currency values and menu linguistics, Lenin and the whole Council of People's Commissaries may possibly have been waiting in suspense for that mysterious package. But patience! The package and we were flying on.

From Kovno we had to make a wide detour toward Dvinsk in order not to contaminate the atmosphere of Poland. The Poles fire at every German or Russian airplane that crosses their border, be it only for half a metre. They know what they are about. The growing intimacy between Russia and Germany constitutes a real peril for their country. And the Pole naturally resents this — and shoots at passenger airplanes. Direct action is best! At Drissa several bullets struck the wings of our plane, but luckily missed the motor.

From Dvinsk to Smolensk there is an unbroken series of still visible trenches, to remind one of the bloody battles of the last war. We flew over Vitebsk and then over Polotsk. Detachments of the Red Army were drilling on the parade grounds. Political problems seem simpler from the air than down on the solid grounds. A Red regiment drilling looked like a child's toy.

After three hours and a half of steady flying we reached Smolensk. The red Soviet star was painted on the barracks and the airplanes. Russian was spoken everywhere. But we were to go no farther that day. The weather was too thick. 'To-morrow you'll be in Moscow, sure.' This time it was our German pilot who said it.

Many of our German aviators have emigrated to Russia and are apparently happy there. They keep the service between Konigsberg and Moscow going, no matter what happens. World sailors! Hard-knit, strong-nerved, but at the same time dreamy and visionary men. Heiler, our pilot, performed some of the most daring air-exploits recorded in the war, and has lighted on one of the highest peaks in Europe. When I asked him why he had tried the latter feat, he merely shrugged his shoulders and said: 'Oh, I had always intended to do so.' A true world sailor. The aviators at Smolensk live in miserable barracks that they themselves have painted and carpeted. Evenings they play on the guitar and sing. Mornings they fly away into the world. It was an inspiring experience to spend a few hours among such men as these.

The next morning I regretted leaving my companions of the evening before. But we were off in a straight line from Moscow. Half way there we flew over the battlefield of Borodino. A century ago a hundred thousand men were slaughtered here. Why must we have battlefields over the whole world? On this leg of our trip we met a number of airplanes going in the opposite direction; although they passed us at a distance of only five hundred to one thousand metres, they were out of sight in a few seconds. Our speed was impressively demonstrated by that fact.

Finally, we could distinguish in the distance, as though it was floating in the air, the golden dome of the Church of the Redeemer. Moscow herself was still invisible, but soon her outlines appeared dimly through the haze. We landed smoothly on the Khodynskoe field. Although we had been four days on the trip, we had spent only eight hours in the air. An automobile from the Foreign Office was on hand to take the courier sack, including the package with the seven seals.

# A CHRISTIAN REFUGE AND ISLAMIC AMBITIONS

## BY COLIN ROSS

[*Colin Ross, whose Persian sketches we recently published in the* Living Age, *returned from Asia, Armenia, and the Caucasus shortly before the Turks won their recent victory. The accounts of the impressions he gathered in Armenia and Mohammedan Asia that we publish below are from the* Vossische Zeitung *of October 26 and November 5; and the* Neue Freie Presse, *of October 29.*]

### I

THE ARCHBISHOP OF ERIVAN said in an agitated voice: 'During the early days of Bolshevist rule I stood on this terrace every night, and lifting my arms to Heaven cried out: "How long, O Lord, holy and true, dost thou not judge and avenge our blood!"'

One side of the archepiscopal palace hangs over the cliff like an eagle's nest. Immediately below the terrace, which is some twenty feet wide, the cliff is perpendicular. Far below a mountain torrent winds its way with many a foaming rapid through a rocky cañon. Little huts cling like swallows' nests to the distant cliffs. On the left, the ruins of some proud building of the days of Persian rule crown a lofty precipice.

A road winds with many tortuous turns and bends down to the river. Tawny boys are bathing under the high arches of the bridge. Along the opposite bank stretch garden after garden and orchards and vineyards heavily laden with fruit. The boughs of the fruit trees are bent to the earth with their luscious burden, as if bowing humbly for our blessing. And far beyond, across the river and gardens and the remoter highlands, there rises clear, icily distinct and imposing in the distance, the great mass of Mount Ararat. Even were it not for the legend that Noah's Ark rested here after the Deluge — in the treasure house of the cloister Etschmiadsin authentic pieces of the Ark are still exhibited — it is a mountain of impressive majesty. In the clear atmosphere the mountain seems almost at hand's reach from us. We are conscious of standing in the immediate presence of an impersonation of nature's lonely grandeur. This is a place that makes you feel nearer the All High. The Archbishop appreciates my feeling and leaves me silently to my thoughts.

A little later the chief of the American Relief Mission joins me on the terrace. During the last few days I have been about much with this gentleman, visiting refugee shelters, work places, hospitals and — more numerous than all else — orphanages.

It is a mighty labor of self-sacrificing love for their fellow men that the Americans have performed in Armenia. From every point of the compass Armenian refugees have fled to this little territory, that they call their own — a territory that was never able to feed even the original population. Indescribable misery and certain starvation would have followed had not the Americans promptly taken a hand. Their representatives receive the fugitives as soon as they arrive, provide them with shelter, food, and clothing, and wherever possible, with productive labor.

But above all they have gathered together the deserted and famished orphans from the streets — tens of thousands of them whose parents were massacred or died of pest and famine. All over Armenia these orphans are being fed, clothed and educated by the Americans. At Alexandropol forty thousand of them have been sheltered in one old military post.

Most of the boys are dressed in Boy Scout uniforms. They live with their Scout-masters and are taught to take care of themselves so far as possible. They have their own gardens that they cultivate, the produce of which belongs to them. They cook their own food, wash their own clothing, and perform other services around their quarters. They are also drilled daily under the folds of a great American flag, to the music of a military band, likewise composed of Boy Scouts. The head of the relief detachment in Erivan is personally the very incarnation of pacifism and gentleness, but he is tremendously enthusiastic over the military features of this education. He just stepped in to have me observe these scouts, who were drilling in an open field across the river, almost under the shadow of Mount Ararat.

The American formations were soon joined by others. The English Relief Mission also has its Boy Scouts and Girl Scouts, whose brown uniforms were soon visible on the parade ground with the white uniforms of the Americans. The Union Jack was flying side by side with the Stars and Stripes. Then, last of all, the Bolshevist Boy Scouts arrived, distinguished from the others by their bright red cravats and their bright red banner. The three groups drilled together in good fellowship and good comradery, under the command of the 'American' Scout-master. This 'American' is a Turkish Armenian, who served as a Lieutenant in the Osman Army during the World War.

I watched the exercises with a feeling of deep skepticism in my heart. This did not seem to me the way to smooth over the conflicts that agitate Armenia, Transcaucasia, and all Western Asia. The noble and unselfish work that the Americans are doing here has not been spared hostile criticism.

Had it not been for the Americans, the Armenians would have starved, and yet many view the Stars and Stripes — which the Yankees, I must confess, display on every possible occasion — with mixed feelings. The Armenian Government itself pursues a policy of pin-pricks toward the American Relief Mission. It does not forward the Mission's mail promptly; it makes difficulty over the passports of the American Relief workers; it insists on being paid for the electric current it supplies to light the Mission's buildings, hospitals, schools, and shelters, and occasionally cuts off the current.

Even though we are standing under the shadow of Ararat, where the Ark of Noah landed and God spanned the heavens with a rainbow in sign of his propitiated wrath, the soil beneath our feet is sown thickly with the seed of bloody feuds.

But just as this thought strikes me I feel a hand on my arm. The Archbishop's gaze is fixed aloft on the mountain summit. Heavy rain clouds have clustered around the peak through which the sun is shooting its declining shafts. And behold, as we watch, the brilliant bow springs from the foot of Ararat and loses itself in the breaking clouds above.

There is a great waving of flags on the parade ground below. Bands are playing, and the shrill cheering of children's voices rises to our ears. The American at my side snatches off his hat in enthusiasm, and waves it to the children below with a triple 'Hip hip hurrah!' But the Archbishop on my right stretches his arm out toward Ararat, and murmurs in a low voice, as if to himself, instead of to me: —

'I do set my bow in the cloud, and it shall be for a token of a covenant between me and the earth.'

II

I MET Ali Kemal, the brother of Djemal Pasha, at Kushka, a sun-baked city on the Afghan-Russian frontier. Djemal himself had been a Turkish army commander during the war, and later Minister of War in Afghanistan. He had left for Moscow where he had negotiations in hand with the Soviet Government, and his brother, who was organizing a model cavalry regiment in Afghanistan, had accompanied him. I had letters of recommendation to Djemal himself, whose tragic assassination at Tiflis was unknown to either of us. They served to secure the confidence of his brother and we speedily became excellent friends.

Ali Kemal had been on horseback for several weeks, accompanying his brother on his journey from Kabul. Kushka was the first place where he had stopped to rest. The fact that he had a brief period of leisure, and that the desolate little frontier post afforded him no other companionship than my own, probably made him more communicative than he otherwise might have been.

I had become more or less familiar with the interplay of intrigue and rivalry that spreads like a network through the Islamic world, during my sojourn in the Ukraine, the Caucasus, and Persia. Defeat had not been an unmitigated misfortune for the Osman Turks. Before the war the other Mohammedan races had resented their rule, and the Arabs, in particular, were inclined to dispute their primacy even with the sword. This hostility has now vanished. In the first place, the Turks are no longer political superiors, and with the removal of the resentment their former supremacy caused, the feeling that they are brothers of the same faith has been strengthened. Furthermore, the brilliant hopes that the Arabs cherished after Turkish defeat have not been realized. They have merely exchanged Turkish rule for British rule. They regard the government of Emir Feisal, set up over them by English bayonets, a farce; and resent it more than outright British rule. Mesopotamia is seething with suppressed revolt; and though the Arabs are not good soldiers, their practically independent desert tribes are abundantly provided with rifles, machine guns, and even artillery. The Indian Mohammedan troops that Great Britain had on the Euphrates and Tigris at the time of my visit made no secret of the fact that they would not fight their fellow believers, if it came to a new war.

The Turks now have an understanding with the Arabs and also with the Kurds, who are fighting to free themselves from the Persians. Their relations with Persia proper are precarious, if not actually hostile. The antagonism of the two peoples is due partly to the doctrinal controversy between the Sunnites and the Shiites, and partly to the Kurdish question. Consequently the Angora government had no representative at Teheran. The only Turkish officer there at the time of my visit was a chargé d'affaires representing the Sultan's government in Constantinople. So Angora's lines of communication were through the Caucasus and Turkestan to Afghanistan. All along this route Turkish emissaries were welcomed with great cordiality, for part of the Afghans, and the Tartars who dwell in the original home of the Osman

Turks, speak a dialect of their language. Turkish coins, and even Turkish paper money, are in common use clear through to the Afghan border.

The resources of the Angora government were decidedly limited. In spite of all the assistance and supplies they received from the Russians and from the French, they lacked most of the things needed for a campaign. Kemal Pasha owes his later military success primarily to geographical advantages, to the extraordinary endurance and devotion of the Anatolian soldiers, and to the weakness and demoralization of his Greek opponents.

Kemal presumed for a moment to defy the power of England, because he believed he had the whole Islamic world, as well as Russia and the Ukraine, behind him. And Russia is not an ally to be despised. No matter how powerful the Nationalist movement is that is sweeping through the Islamic nations to-day, the military training of the Mohammedan peoples and their equipment for modern warfare — if we except the Turks — are totally inadequate for a successful appeal to battle against the Great Powers of Europe.

Soviet Russia in a certain sense made possible the pan-Islamic movement. This was not solely by supporting the Turks. The Bolshevist revolution liberated the Mohammedans of Central Asia from the iron rule of the Tsars' government, and taught them to aspire to national independence. The purpose of Soviet Russia in encouraging these new ideas was to convert its Mohammedan subjects to Bolshevism, and to spread the Bolshevist movement to the neighboring Islamic states of Turkey, Persia, Afghanistan, and even India, where this could be used as a weapon against England. In Turkestan, the Soviet Government went so far as to prefer the natives to the Russian settlers themselves. The officials in Turkestan, Bokhara, and Khiva are almost exclusively native Mohammedans. Azerbaijan, in the Eastern Caucasus, is a Mohammedan republic practically independent of Moscow. Everywhere throughout these countries Friday is the legal holiday. The Arabic alphabet is in use, and Mohammedan law is in force.

The idea of the Communists was to exalt Internationalism over Nationalism, but it is doubtful if this has been the result. It would take a long article even to outline the relations between Islam and Bolshevism. They have much in common, and, at the same time, much that is irreconcilable. But whatever the outcome of their mutual contact, there is a general awakening throughout Asia. Afghanistan, India's next-door neighbor, is filled with a burning ambition to become a second Japan in her mountain fastnesses.

III

I looked forward with some trepidation to my journey during the hot season into Turkestan, for I was still suffering from an attack of malaria. Further, the Bolsheviki placed many difficulties in my way, because Turkestan was in a state of turmoil and the campaign against Enver Pasha was in full swing. Finally, however, all obstacles were overcome. I crossed the Caspian Sea, and zigzagged via Merv through the Black Sand Desert to the Afghan border. At Merv I was unexpectedly detained because a cholera epidemic was raging; and I was not permitted to proceed until I had been quarantined and repeatedly inoculated. I proceeded to Kushka, Bokhara, Samarkand, the old headquarters of Tamerlane, and lastly to Tashkent, from which point I crossed the Aral Sea and reached Moscow via Orenberg.

Even before the war such a trip was no pleasure excursion. After war and revolution have left their wreckage everywhere, the difficulties are immeasurably greater. Turkestan was in open revolt. Bandits were robbing and murdering throughout the Caucasus. Enver Pasha's supporters were fighting the Bolsheviki. I traveled as a man must have traveled in the Middle Ages, not knowing what perilous adventure might be awaiting me behind every strip of forest and every cliff. Upon the whole, this was the most dangerous journey I have ever made.

It is not easy to describe the picturesque variety and contrasts of such a country, where the bloody romance of revolution has been imposed upon the dreamy reveries of the Orient; where scenes from 'The Night Refuge' abruptly alternate with scenes from the Arabian Nights; sleeping one night in a miserable clay hut by the side of a caravan route, and the next night in an Oriental palace set in the midst of a glorious garden; and with all this, never knowing what the next day would bring forth, living in a land of outlaws, speculating constantly on what was to happen next. Such an existence is exciting and stimulating, but more fatiguing than the most arduous bodily toil.

All Central Asia is in a ferment. The Bolshevist revolution has swept away every familiar dyke and barrier that confined its fluid peoples. The reciprocal relations of Bolshevism and Islamism are still undefined and their ultimate result is beyond present prediction. The adherents of these two movements are brought together mainly by their common hatred of England. That alone enables them to tolerate their mutual differences. This is the moving force behind the rapprochement of Russia with the Turks, Persians, and Afghans. It is not unlikely, however, that in the back of the Turkish and the Afghan mind lurks a plan to dispense with Russia as soon as England is removed from the field.

The peoples of Central Asia are determined to free themselves from all European tutelage, whatever its source. This explains why Moscow, in spite of its conciliatory policy, is now fighting a serious insurrection in Turkestan and Bokhara. It is sending courier after courier across the Afghan mountains and the Pamir plateau to sow seed of discontent in India.

The Indian situation seems far more dangerous when viewed from Central Asia than when viewed from Europe. We cannot tell when the storm will break in that country, but all indications point to an early date. That will be the test. Then we shall know whether the latent differences between Islamism and Bolshevism, between Sunnites and Shiites, between Angora and Teheran, between Kemal Pasha and Enver Pasha, will prove serious enough to save England.

# ROUGET DE LISLE AND THE MARSEILLAISE

## BY EDOUARD GACHOT

From *Figaro*, October 29
(LIBERAL NATIONALIST DAILY)

WHAT name of poet, musician, and officer is there to compare with that of Rouget de Lisle? The soldiers of the 'Year II,' who were beginning anew a Roman epic, hailed in him the bard of ancient times. Brunswick had the holy hymn translated at Verdun. The King of Prussia, halted before Mayence, said to Kalreuth: 'The *Marseillaise* is worth two armies to our enemies'; for it was especially against the German princes that the French poet had thundered in strophes flaming with his anger. An aristocrat and once an adherent of the King, this Jurassian had become a citizen at the altar of a threatened fatherland.

The true history of his words and deeds has been distorted. He made pretension neither to the glory of an Anacreon nor to the fortune of a Voltaire. The son of a lawyer in the Parliament, born at Lons-le-Saunier May 10, 1760, godson of the famous Gertrude de la Tour, the sister of the pastel painter, he was to don at twenty-two the uniform of a second lieutenant, and to serve the monarchy for seven years as an officer of pioneers. Not being a member of any coterie, without protection in high places, Rouget de Lisle was not dismayed at the change of régime. A poor man, he turned to his muse and to his violin for those distractions which so often offer a means of salvation from the violence of passion.

Becoming a lieutenant September 7, 1789, as a member of the garrison of Neuf-Brisach, he was neither surprised nor disturbed by the declaration of war, which was transmitted by a Girondin minister on April 20, 1792. The destiny of a freed people was to be decided in the smoke of cannon. Alsace was to see again the warlike days of a Turenne and a Montecuccoli. The various French cohorts were to take their stand once more on the left bank of the Rhine to halt the onslaughts of the Suevi under a new Ariovistus. Such were the circumstances that called Rouget de Lisle, now promoted to a captaincy, to Strassburg on January 3, 1792.

At that time one man was the dominating and inspiring force among the people of Strassburg — Frederic Philippe, Baron de Dietrich, an enlightened official who had declined the ancient Teutonic title of *Ammeister* for that of *maire* — a mineralogist, the author of a volume on *Des forges et des salines des Pyrénées* — a man who had given himself entirely to the tasks of freedom. His patriotic ardor inevitably brought him into the society of the army officers. Knowing that in June the garrison was to form a wing of Luckner's army, Dietrich set himself to organize a farewell festival. Here gathered the centurions of the new legions, contemptuous of the warlike to-morrow, which might, perchance, be fatal; here, too, were those who saw nothing before them save new Champs Catalauniques. These were the men who knew that on the shoulders of the King of Prussia lay the red mantle of Attila the Hun. They grew quietly attentive as Dietrich made a suggestion to his guests: —

'We need, messieurs, a war song with which to march against the enemy. Who will compose it?'

Lapiète, a lieutenant, turned to Rouget: —

'Poet, call back the song of Leonidas and his Spartans.'

Rouget de Lisle left the gathering abruptly. He walked straight to his quarters, along streets half blocked with cannon, and among the soldiers grouped in front of the doors. When he reached his modest dwelling, in the rue de la Mésange, the captain lighted his lamp and sat down at a little desk. Under the spell of an overmastering inspiration he wrote some couplets, and then, taking down his violin, began to play stirring music. When dawn broke the immortal song was finished. The composer, in the throes of feverish emotion, never thought of rest. He hurried off to read his poem to Dietrich — not to sing it to the accompaniment of a harpsichord, as the plates and pictures of the time show the scene. At noon that day, before three battalions drawn up on the parade ground, Rouget de Lisle sang the new song, and a wild enthusiasm seized upon all those who heard him. But this *Chant de l' armée du Rhin*, which was printed by the *Journal de Strasbourg*, was forbidden by some of the generals, who found its expressions a little too daring.

Carried to Marseille and sung there, it was adopted — though in modified form — by the people, and then carried to Paris, where on July 30, 1792, it created excitement at an evening banquet given in the *Grand Salon du Couronnement de la Constitution*, the principal restaurant on the Champs Élysées. The new refrain ran: —

*Nos armes, citoyens, ont triomphé des rois.*
*Veillons! veillons! sans nous lasser, au maintien*
*de nos droits.*

At the *fête civique* of October 14 a new stanza was added: —

*Français qu'un même vœu rassemble*
*Pour être heureux, soyons unis,*
*Ne formons tous qu'un grand ensemble,*
*Notre salut en est le prix.*
*Que de la République entière*
*Chacun de nous soit le soutien,*
*Dans tous voyons le citoyen,*
*Et dans le citoyen un frère.*

From Paris the song spread to the armies, where it was favored by the leaders, and the first version was once more adopted. Rouget, no doubt, profited by the widespread popularity of his work? No, his name was placed on the list of suspects. Dietrich had already been arrested for protesting against the crimes of August 10. He was being dragged to trial when Rouget, busy with his military duties, gave a little bread to a homeless woman, sixty years old, who had fallen exhausted near the camp. She was the mother of an emigré. Féroul, the people's commissioner attached to the army, suspended the officer from service on August 25. Restored to duty September 16 and serving with General Vence, he distinguished himself for bravery at the siege of Namur. After the surrender on December 2, he was sent to Strassburg.

On March 15, 1793, Carnot required an oath of obedience to the Convention, from the Army of the Rhine. Among numerous cases of passive obedience, there were also vigorous refusals. Rouget de Lisle declared that he loved France and served her faithfully, but not the power that had thrown Dietrich into chains. Carnot insisted.

'You have recognized the national colors. To-day the Convention holds them, and is the State.'

'I am only the enemy of our enemies.'

'Will you compel me to strip you of your rank for hostility to the State — you, the author of the *Marseillaise?*'

'I will endure any trials that may come to me.'

Carnot contented himself with demanding his discharge. Rouget went back to his lodgings on the rue de la Mésange. Féraud prepared an accusation against the 'conspirator.' Euloge Schneider, the man who had insisted on covering the weather vane on the Strassburg cathedral with a red liberty-cap, added other charges. The poet was taken under arrest to Paris and cast into a dungeon at the Conciergerie; and, by the irony of circumstance, on the very day after his imprisonment one of Santerre's battalions passed, singing the *Marseillaise*.

Freed after the execution of Robespierre, Rouget de Lisle was offered the friendship of Hoche, who had also been persecuted by the terrorists, and who enrolled him among his own aides-de-camp, August 14, 1893; and as an officer in the Cherbourg army Rouget received a wound at Quiberon. His health was failing, and though given command of a battalion March 2, 1796, he was compelled to leave the service on May 1, when his song had just begun to resound beyond the Rhine.

Suddenly those virile tones were silenced. The Consular régime had given direction that the song should not be heard. Only the old soldiers of Fleurus remembered to hum it under their breath — after they had been discharged. At Moscow, in 1812, among the smoking ruins of the city of the Tsars, a shout of *Aux armes, citoyens*, was heard, and in the frozen water of the Berezina the engineers of the Zabern company, who were building a bridge under the very eye of Napoleon himself, took up the song: —

*Allons, enfants de la patrie,*
*Le jour de gloire est arrivé.*

Napoleon lifted his hat to the heroic men, and when Berthier ventured to protest against the forbidden song, remarked: —

'Let these gallant fellows recall our days of glory if they want to.'

Meantime, in his little house at Choisy-le-Roi, the composer was consoling himself for the inconstancy of men and the forgetfulness of sovereigns by playing his violin and writing his lyric tragedy, *Macbeth*. He died in 1836, but his name and his war song have endured the storms of a century.

We felt it fitting, on July 14, to bear his ashes to the Pantheon. Why should we not insist on seeking out the house where Dietrich dwelt in 1792, and why should we not erect on the Kehl bridge, facing that Germany whose tyrants he assailed, the statue of our modern Pindar? The echoes of a French Rhine would take up the voices of the pilgrims, who would come on patriotic journeys to repeat at the monument's foot the strophes of our nation's song.

# THE AUGUSTAN AGE OF SCIENCE

## BY SIR RICHARD GREGORY

[*Sir Richard Gregory is editor of* Nature, *the most important British scientific journal. He is the son of the poet, John Gregory, who died a few months ago. A recent article of Sir Richard's which appeared in* Nature *finds an echo in the concluding paragraph of the present study. At that time he suggested that scientific men must adopt means to prevent the abuse and employment for unworthy ends of the discoveries that they had made — a suggestion which called forth much comment in the British press.*]

From the *Sunday Times*, October 22
(INDEPENDENT JOURNAL)

EVERY scientific discovery is a possible factor of industrial or intellectual development — a new tint which may change the color of the whole landscape, but meaningless until on the canvas. A chronological list of such discoveries recorded in unrelated succession would be easy to make, but would fail to show the points of contact of Science with the living world — the new social circumstances and expansive thought created by new contributions to natural knowledge. Through these revelations during the past hundred years or so conditions of life and views as to the history of the earth and of man have undergone more revolutionary changes than in all the ages preceding them; and it is mainly to them that we propose here to devote attention.

Beginning with the earth itself, a century ago Archbishop Ussher's chronology, which assigned the creation of the world to the year 4004 B.C., was still generally accepted, though dissatisfaction with it had been expressed. All terrestrial changes were attributed to the Deluge or other catastrophes, until Lyell produced evidence in his *Principles of Geology*, published in 1830, that slow evolution rather than sudden revolution is the process by which Nature sculptures the surface of our globe.

The final blow to the old foundations of belief as to the age of the earth and of man came with the discovery of a new world of ancient life buried in the rocks, and associated in some places with man's own handiwork. Gigantic reptilian creatures of former days, such as the ichthyosaurus and plesiosaurus, were found in 1821, and in the same year the bones of elephants, rhinoceroses, hippopotami, hyenas, and other animals long extinct in these islands were identified from remains recovered from beds under the floor of a cave at Kirkdale. Curiously-shaped flints had long before been found with similar relics of past ages, but their origin was not understood. Recognition that they were tools and weapons of early man came shortly after the middle of the last century, as the result of a critical examination of well-made flint implements found by M. Boucher de Perthes near Abbeville and Amiens fifteen years earlier. The conviction was then forced upon geologists that man was a contemporary of the mammoth, the woolly-haired rhinoceros, cave-bear, cave-hyena, and other extinct animals about thirty thousand years ago.

It thus became no longer possible to believe that man belonged only to the latest order of geological events, and had always been of the present type.

# THE AUGUSTAN AGE OF SCIENCE

He had evidently a prehistoric ancestry, the earliest known form of which is now believed to be represented by the remains of a walking or 'ground' ape — as distinct from apes which live in trees — found at Trinil, in Java, toward the end of the nineteenth century in deposits laid down before the first glacial age, probably about half a million years ago. Ape-like characteristics appear in the remains of a skull found at Piltdown, Sussex, in 1912, and in a massive lower jaw from a deposit near Heidelberg, and their age may be anything from 100,000 to 500,000 years. Types of the direct progenitor of modern man are represented by the skull and bones found in a cave in the Neanderthal, near Düsseldorf, about sixty years ago, and a fine skeleton from the grotto of La-Chapelle-aux-Saints, in the Dordogne, France, secured in 1908. Through the fifty thousand years or so from the end of the last glacial age to the present time there is an unbroken chain of evidence of human development.

The appearance of Darwin's *Origin of Species* in 1859, followed by his *Descent of Man* in 1871, finally disposed of the doctrine of special creation of man and other living things in their existing structures and shapes, and substituted for it the theory of progressive development throughout succeeding ages. Conceptions of evolution in organic nature had been held long before, and what Darwin did was not only to marshal overwhelming evidence in support of the fact itself, but also to show how variations combined with the ever-present struggle for existence almost inevitably causes extinction of the less improved forms of life and leads to diversities of character to be transmitted to new generations.

What is true for animate nature generally is true also for man, who had thus to regard himself not as shaped once for all in a mould broken six thousand years ago, but as having branched out from an ancestral stock through the possession and survival of the distinctive characters and capacities by which he has made himself lord of creation and master of his own destiny. By the principles of evolution life becomes dynamic instead of static — a process of movement onward and upward, instead of a descent from a Golden Age or a condition of knowledge which could never be regained in this world.

It is not now possible to doubt organic evolution as a fact, or that natural selection is the main formative factor in sifting the fit from the unfit under any particular conditions of existence. Exactly how the earliest forms of life arose, how new types developed, and how their specific capacities are transmitted from one generation to another are, however, still subjects of acute discussion among biologists, and are likely to be for many years yet. The principles of Mendelism, upon which so much useful work has been done since 1900, when they became known, though they were discovered by Mendel so long ago as 1866, provide practical rules as to the regulation of the inheritances of biological characteristics, but their interpretation is another matter. The ovum from which a human being develops after fertilization does not differ in any observable characters from the ova of other creatures, and in the early stages of growth the embryos of vertebrate animals cannot be distinguished one from another, though one may eventually become a rabbit and the other a child.

A century ago nothing was known of the actual changes which an ovum undergoes when it is fertilized, for it was not until 1843 that the effect of the union of spermatozoa with ova was observed in the case of a rabbit. But though the changes which follow fertilization of an ovum can be seen and traced through all the stages of embryonie development to birth — a multicellular vertebrate animal, for example, from a minute fertilized egg — only in a few forms of life are observable structures in the cell associated with characters developed in the future organism; and even in these cases the evidence is not convincing. It is assumed that some quality or structure of the simple cell is continuous from one generation to another, and carries with it particular hereditary characters, but what this germplasm, as Weismann named it, actually is remains still to be determined. What we do know is that the human ovum does not contain a model in miniature of the future offspring, as the 'animalculists' had contended for centuries before von Baer, in 1828, discovered and described an ovum about one two-hundredth of an inch in diameter. Man, like other vertebrate animals, begins his individual existence in the form of a single cell or fertilized egg, which by repeated divisions, each giving rise to a new generation of cells, develops into the adult organism.

Embryology became a science through Darwin's work on evolution, which has indeed been the fertilizing principle of most studies of organic life during the past sixty years. Its basis is the cell or elementary vital unit upon which all organic growth and development depend. As now understood by biologists, a cell is not a box of a particular shape, like the cells of a honeycomb, but the substance in the box, and the problems it presents are so complicated and important that a new science — cytology — has marked them off as its concern. The semi-transparent protoplasm within a cell is the actual living substance of the organism, and is the common basis of all animal and plant tissues. The centre of activity governing the vital functions of the cell is the nucleus, discovered and named by Robert Brown in 1831. Following up this observation, M. J. Schleiden and T. Schwann in 1839 published their epoch-making work on the cell theory, which has developed into a most important biological generalization. The speck of protoplasm with its nucleus has proved to be the physical basis of life.

It was by a natural transition that Schwann passed from microscopic studies of the cell to observations of minute organisms and their place in the economy of Nature. He reached the conclusion, for example, that fermentation was due to the growth of the vegetable organisms, rediscovered by him in 1837, which form yeast, and that putrefaction might be due to a similar cause. These views werè, however, so strongly opposed at the time that they found few supporters, and it was not until twenty years later that Pasteur proved beyond all question that there could be neither alcoholic fermentation nor putrefying matter in the absence of microorganisms. The significance of bacteria in disease was established in 1860 by the recognition of a microscopic plant as being the true cause of anthrax; and since then modern medicine has been largely concerned in detecting, isolating, and combating the invisible foes associated with many common diseases — typhoid, diphtheria, dysentery, tetanus, cholera, plague, and others.

The science of bacteriology did not exist a century ago. It was then believed that there could be spontaneous generation of living organisms, but Pasteur showed conclusively that such organisms were never actually created, but grew from others; and he further proved that particular forms of germs were the causes of putrefaction. Following up this conclusion, Lister applied it in 1866 to the treatment of wounds, and showed that the exclusion of the microscopic living causes of decomposition meant the disappearance of hospital fevers such as pyæmia, gangrene, and so on, which previously exacted fearful toll from patients submitted to surgical operation. Antiseptic and aseptic methods had previously been introduced with success by Semmelweis in the maternity wards of a great hospital in Vienna, but it was Pasteur who discovered the minute organism associated with puerperal fever, to which so many women succumbed, and it was upon the sure foundation of Pasteur's researches that Lister based his methods of preventing septic troubles. Antiseptic treatment and the use of anæsthetics, administered first as sulphuric ether in the United States in 1844, and later in the form of chloroform in England, opened up a greatly increased range of surgical operations, and have been the means of avoiding untold suffering as well as saving hundreds of thousands of human lives.

Clearly associated with the science of bacteriology, the founders of which were Pasteur, Koch, and Lister, is that of parasitology, which is of relatively recent growth and is concerned chiefly with diseases due to particular parasites — neither bacteria nor bacilli. Laveran discovered in 1880 that malarial fever is caused by millions of minute animal parasites, and it was suggested by him and Koch that the malarial germ is carried by mosquitoes. Manson carried this suggestion further about 1894, but it was left to Ronald Ross to establish the theory by a long series of difficult experiments. Both malaria and yellow fever were banished from Havana by destroying the breeding-places of mosquitoes. The construction of the Panama Canal became possible by the adoption of these measures, and many other places in which these diseases were formerly rampant have similarly been made healthy for white people. The Black Death, or plague, is another insect-borne disease, proved in 1894 by two Japanese doctors — Yersin and Kitasato — to be caused by a minute vegetable parasite conveyed by fleas from rats to men. Sleeping sickness is conveyed by the tsetse fly, typhus fever by lice, and other diseases by other insects; it is only when the true causative organisms and their carrying agents have been discovered that preventive measures can be employed with the assurance of success.

Much of modern scientific progress is indeed based upon the study of minute things and their effects. In the human body disorder of a single organ will disturb the working of the whole mechanism. Each organ is not isolated, but correlated with others, and through its internal secretions determines conditions of disease or health, of growth, physical characteristics, and development generally. Even in diet minute amounts of substances known as vitamins are essential to nutrition in addition to the proteins, fats, carbohydrates, and mineral salts which are the common constituents of foods. Beri-beri, for example, is a deficiency disease caused by the consumption of rice from which the necessary nutritive vitamins have been removed in the polishing process of milling, and rickets are associated with the absence of a vitamin which occurs in abundance in cod-liver oil and butter. Margarine must have this vitamin added to it if it is to be a nutritious food.

In the manufacture of this butter-substitute use is made of the property which minute quantities of certain substances possess of promoting chemical changes in other substances. At the beginning of this century it was discovered that oils like olive oil could be converted into solid fats if sprayed into a vessel containing hydrogen gas and some finely divided nickel, which acts as a 'catalyst,' but itself remains unaltered. Any degree of hardening of a fatty oil can be obtained by lengthening the time of this process of hydrogenation, and the objectionable odors of fish oils and other low-class fats can be completely removed. Chemical industries depend largely upon facilitating the divorce of some elements and their reunion with others, and in this transformation the presence of the impassive catalytic agent often plays an essential part.

All substances — organic as well as inorganic — are made up of chemical elements, of which ninety or so are now recognized, about thirty of which have been discovered during the past century. It was formerly supposed that organic compounds could be procured only through the agency of 'vital forces,' but when Wöhler succeeded in 1828 in synthesizing carbamide — previously known solely as the product of vital action — and acetic acid and other organic compounds were afterwards artificially produced from their constituent elements, the doctrine of vital force in chemistry was broken down. Since then thousands of similar products have been produced for everyday use, as dyes, drugs, perfumes, photographic chemicals, and for other purposes. The waste coal-tar, which was an annoying by-product of the manufacture of illuminating gas in the first half of the nineteenth century, proved to be a mine of wealth to synthetic chemistry, beginning with the discovery of mauve, the first aniline dye, by Perkin in 1856, and now producing substances worth tens of millions annually.

Lighting by coal-gas had established itself a century ago, but little improvement was made in it until the incandescent mantle was introduced by Auer von Welsbach in 1880. The two elements, thorium and cerium, which enter into the constitution of these mantles were discovered many years earlier, and had no useful application before they entered into the gas industry. Cerium itself seems to act as a catalytic agent in facilitating combustion, for only about one per cent is used in gas mantles, and no advantage is gained by increasing or decreasing this small proportion. Calcium carbide, from which another illuminant — acetylene gas — was later produced, was made by Wöhler in 1862, and has become a commercial product of prime importance.

The incandescent mantle saved the gas industry at a time when electricity had become a serious competitor as a means of lighting. Faraday had shown in 1831 that a moving magnet produced an electric current in a coil of wire near it, a discovery upon which the construction of every electric dynamo depends. There never was an observation which has had greater industrial and social influence. Every electric supply station, and every practical use of electric power, has its origin in Faraday's researches on magneto electricity. It took nearly fifty years for the discovery that mechanical movement could create an electric current to be applied to the construction of an effective dynamo, and we did not take the lead in this, as we did with the steam engine, but let Germany, the United States, and other countries occupy the field which Faraday, Wheatstone, Kelvin, and other British men of science had opened, and we entered it only after they had shown its fertility.

No advances in electrical or other machines and engineering structures would, however, have been possible in the absence of the developments of steel manufacture which began about fifty years ago. Of particular importance was the discovery and invention of the extraordinary material and alloy —

manganese steel — by Sir Robert Hadfield in the 'eighties of the last century, followed up by the production of nickel steel, chromium steel, aluminium steel, and others. Dozens of similar alloy-steels are now known, each with specific properties, and one or more of them are used in the construction of every motor-car, aeroplane, projectile, armor-plate, tramway crossing, machine tool or other product of modern engineering.

Aluminium, one of the substances used in alloy-steel, was not discovered until 1828, though it is the most widely distributed element on the earth. Nearly two hundred thousand tons of the metal are now produced annually, entirely by electrical methods.

We are indeed in the age of steel and electricity, and the greatest marvels in the history of the world, due to their use, are now accepted as matters of everyday life. The metallic filament incandescent electric lamp, slightly modified, has been found to be the most sensitive detector of electric waves used to transmit messages by wireless telegraphy and telephony. By its use speech can be heard for a distance of a couple of thousand miles and signals detected from the ends of the earth. An electric telegraph line eight miles long was laid down by Ronalds at Hammersmith in 1816; twenty years later it came into general use in England; and in another twenty years a cable had been laid across the Atlantic; but all these applications of the electric current were obvious in comparison with the use of electric waves for transmitting signals and speech. When Graham Bell produced his telephone in 1876 the world was astonished at the wonderful powers of the new instrument; but we are now on the threshold of a far more marvelous achievement, and there is every reason to believe that before long it will be possible to converse between London and New York or Cape Town as readily as a conversation can now be held by ordinary telephonic means between two cities in Great Britain.

The effect of these facilities of communication, like that of improved means of locomotion, has been to make the world smaller than it was a century ago. The Atlantic was crossed in a fortnight in 1833 by a vessel using steam-power alone, and by one using a screw propeller instead of paddles twelve years later. Since then the chief developments have been in size and speed, and in the use of turbines instead of reciprocating engines. Much the same is true of steam traction on railways since Stephenson constructed his engine for the Stockton and Darlington line in 1821, the chief change being the introduction of electric traction for tramways and railways. Improvements in the efficiency of these and all other uses of mechanical power are due to the establishment of the principle of the conservation of energy through the labors of Mayer and Helmholtz in Germany, and Joule and Kelvin in Great Britain. Towards the end of the eighteenth century Lavoisier had proved that throughout all chemical transformations investigated there was never the gain or loss of a single particle of matter; but the fact that energy could also never be created or destroyed was established only by persistent experiment and against much opposition. The principle lies at the basis of the construction of all efficient forms of power transformation, including the internal-combustion engines which have revolutionized communication on highways and made dynamic aviation an everyday affair. Flying machines of much the same type as that of early aeroplanes were designed about a century ago, but it was not until after the invention of the petrol motor that the brothers Wright were able twenty years ago to make sustained mechanical flight practicable.

But though aviation has enabled man to enter into the dominion of the air, he cannot get very far away from the earth's surface on account of the attenuated atmosphere at high altitudes. The commercial production of liquefied gases enables him, however, to carry liquid air or oxygen to breathe when the atmosphere around him is too rare to sustain respiration. It was only towards the end of the last century that such gases as oxygen, nitrogen, and hydrogen were produced in liquid form, and they are now in common use in medicine as well as in industry. Helium gas, which was first liquefied in 1908 at a temperature of about 480 degrees Fahrenheit below the freezing point of water, has a remarkable history. It was observed as an unknown gas in the sun by Sir Norman Lockyer in 1868, and was then given its name. Twenty-six years later it was obtained by Sir William Ramsay from a terrestrial mineral, and was afterwards found to occur in the waters of many springs.

Lockyer detected helium in the sun by the use of the spectroscope, which enables the chemical constitutions of celestial bodies to be determined by analyzing their light. Auguste Comte had declared that it was impossible for anything definite to be learned about the real nature of the stars, but spectrum analysis has shown that in this, as in other cases, it is unwise to define the limits of human achievement. Not only does the spectroscope enable us to discover the elements in the sun and stars and other celestial bodies, but it also provides a means of determining with remarkable precision their movements towards or away from the earth; and by methods recently introduced the distances of hundreds of stars have been found by measurements of photographs of stellar spectra. It was not until 1838 that the distance of a star had been determined with even approximate accuracy, and proved to be about 650,000 times the distance of the sun from the earth. The methods used for such observations were most laborious, and needed extremely accurate measurements over a period of years. The same amount of attention to spectrum photographs can now determine the distances of hundreds of stars instead of a single one. By another accessory to the astronomical telescope the actual diameters of certain stars have been measured at the Mount Wilson Observatory, California, and for the star Betelgeuse the value proved to be 215,000,000 miles. This was predicted by Prof. Eddington and Prof. Russell from purely theoretical considerations, and the deduction ranks with that of the mathematical determination of the place which the planet Neptune should occupy in the sky, before it was actually discovered there in 1846.

Astronomy in recent years has, however, been concerned not alone with the studies of the visible beams from luminous celestial bodies, but with dark stars and other obscure cosmic matter which there is every reason to believe exceed in quantity what can be seen with even the largest telescopes. The range of ether vibrations which affect our sense of vision — from darkest red to deepest violet — is really only one octave out of more than forty now known. The range was extended by photography, the photographic plate or film being sensitive to rays which produce no effect upon our retinas. Fox Talbot became the father of photography when he invented his calotype process in 1839.

When Röntgen rays, which have proved of such wonderful utility in industry as well as in medical science, were discovered in 1895, it was not realized that they, like visible light, are due to vibrations in the omnipresent ether, but far more rapid, and therefore capable of penetrating structures through which longer waves cannot pass. Invisible rays with the same penetrative properties were soon afterwards found to be emitted by uranium and its compounds, and then Mme. Curie and her husband, after a laborious investigation, isolated from pitchblende — a black ore of uranium — the element radium, which is a far more potent source of invisible radiations than any other substance. It continuously gives off gases, which are themselves radioactive, and the two final products of a series of transformations of these gases are helium and lead.

Radium thus provides an example of the spontaneous disintegration of atoms. Sir Joseph Thomson, Sir Ernest Rutherford, and Professor Soddy are chiefly responsible for tracing out and interpreting the atomic changes which occur to bring about these results. An atom is now regarded as a kind of solar system in miniature, with the main part of its mass concentrated at the centre on a minute nucleus of positive electricity, while around it circulates a certain number of electrons, charged with negative electricity. By a series of brilliant investigations H. G. J. Moseléy — who was killed in the Dardanelles — showed that the chemical properties of an element are governed by the number of electrons revolving around a nucleus, and this number is determined by the units of positive charge possessed by the nucleus. This generalization has proved even more productive of developments in chemical research than the announcement by Mendeléeff in 1871 of the periodic law of the classification of elements, which indicated the probable existence and properties of elements afterwards discovered.

In the nucleus of an atom we have an intense source of energy, indicated by the terrific velocity with which particles are expelled in the disintegration of radioactive substances. By bombarding nitrogen gas with these particles Rutherford has been able to convert some of it into hydrogen, thus transforming one element into another. A new and rich land of promise has been entered during the past few years, and the time is probably not far distant when the unbounded energy of the atoms found in it will be made available for all purposes in which power is required — constructive or destructive. Coal and other forms of fuel will not then be needed, and the whole social organization of the civilized world will have to be readjusted to meet the new conditions. Whether men will prove themselves worthy of the argosies of science which will enter their ports is not for us to predict, but upon the result will depend the future destiny of the human race.

# AL WASAL, OR THE MERGER

## BY HILAIRE BELLOC

[*Poet, journalist, novelist, Mr. Belloc is one of the most vigorous figures in the contemporary school of Catholic writers in England. He and Mr. Chesterton do not like modern industrial civilization — a fact which they seize every occasion to make abundantly clear. This satiric little tale is a continuation of Mr. Belloc's last novel,* The Mercy of Allah, *which dealt with a similar theme in a similar way. In a recent reply to Dean Inge, Mr. Belloc corrected some prevalent impressions with regard to his nationality: 'I was brought over here when I was three weeks old. English is my mother tongue. I have learned French as a foreign language, which I cannot yet always write correctly. I have lived in English surroundings from my earliest recollections of home and school. As to my blood, my father was half French and half Irish. . . . I was brought up here by my mother, who is entirely English — Warwickshire and Yorkshire.'*]

From the *New Statesman*, October 7
(LIBERAL LABOR WEEKLY)

'I HAD been in this town not more than three days, my dear nephews,' said Mahmoud, with a benevolent smile, 'when I lit upon one more happy accident whereby (as it seemed to me) Providence might permit me to advance the welfare of my fellow beings. I know not whether the Merciful, the Just, put it in my mind; I only know that for many years the opportunity had lain there patent to every eye (one would think) yet never used. But Allah has his instruments, and he chose me.

'The town stood, I must tell you, upon either bank of a rapid river. This came down from the slopes of the mountains to the north, and sprang, immediately above the northern gate, from two torrents which united their waters to form the main stream. Each of these torrents ran with force down a gorge of its own, the one on the east, the other on the west of the waters-meet. On each stood, at a distance of half-an-hour's slow walk from the city walls, a mill of ancient date, which ground the corn of the citizens and provided them with flour for their bread.

'That called the East Mill belonged to Hakim, a very worthy man, some fifty years of age, who had a plain, simple face, an ample gray beard, and the carriage of a man of substance, neither very wealthy nor embarrassed. All respected him. He was at ease with himself and mankind. He had inherited the mill from his father, and his father before him.

'That called the West Mill belonged to Selim, a very worthy man, some fifty years of age, who had a plain, simple face, an ample gray beard, and the carriage of a man of substance, neither very wealthy nor embarrassed. All respected him. He was at ease with himself and mankind. He had inherited the mill from his father and his father before him.

, 'I had heard of these two mills on the day of my first arrival; and on the third day I heard more of their owners and of their trade — how each did, on the whole, the same amount of business: now one more, now one less, but year in and year out much of a muchness. "The city needs" (said the chief Corn Chandler, of whom I learnt these particulars) "about ten thousand measures of flour in the year, and of these Hakim, one way and another, will grind about five thousand, and Selim, one way and another, about five thousand. Glory be to the Provider, to the Bountiful, who nourishes mankind with harvests."

'Next day I sauntered to the market and, having had these two pointed out to me, I passed carelessly by them, noting inwardly with exactitude their faces and their thoughts — for these their faces were very far from concealing. They were pursuing their trade in a leisurely but sufficient fashion, taking orders from clients for the delivery of flour, purchasing grain, and noting lists of sacks which were to be sent them for grinding on commission. Each seemed to have a group of regular customers, while a smaller body of buyers and sellers would move from one to the other, comparing prices and ultimately deciding to favor now Hakim, now Selim.

'I can hardly tell you (my dear little nephews) how my heart swelled and overflowed with gratitude as I considered their honest, straightforward gestures, their unstrained lips, their ingenuous eyes. I had had so much experience of the wickedness of men that I had almost forgotten such goodness could be in the world. I lost not a moment, but immediately proceeded to a neighboring shrine and there poured out my thanks and implored the aid of Heaven to decide which of the pair I should first engage, when each was as inviting as his fellow. But though I remained in the most earnest wrestling with God for nearly three quarters of an hour, no sign was vouchsafed me.

'I therefore rose with a sigh to submit the issue to chance. I purchased two turnips in the market, named one Hakim, the other Selim, and tossed them together into the air. Hakim first reached the ground. To Hakim, therefore, did I procure an introduction, and, at his courteous suggestion, walked back slowly with him up the torrent side, through the cool of the evening, toward the mountain and his home. We entered the Mill House, loud with the sound of water and delicious with the scent of whole-meal. He entertained me well. We talked of my travels far into the night, and I think I moved him somewhat by my accounts of large sums acquired most rapidly, and of gain without effort. Next day he visited the lodging I had hired in the city. The next I came again to his mill. We were soon fast friends.

'"Hakim," said I to him one day in the next week, as we stood at sunset in his doorway overlooking the city below, "Hakim" (we had been discussing the inexplicable prosperity of the Kadi) "I cannot but believe that a little novelty might honorably add to your revenue."

'"Something of the sort has lately passed through my own mind," he answered, "especially when you spoke the other evening of how the coffee-seller enlarged his trade by generously presenting every buyer with an illuminated text, which, in turn, he was paid by the text-illuminator to distribute as a sample of his skill."

'"Some few of your clients," said I, "visit your mill after meeting you in the market. Now, were these visits rendered in some way specially pleasing, they would increase. New customers would come to you. Your sales of flour would speedily grow."

'Hakim was already convinced. He spent no small sum in putting up a hall, where sweetmeats and sherbet were offered to his guests by the most charming servitors. Later he hired two singers and a fortune-teller. Soon a company of players appeared, whose jests were so familiar that they drew a regular audience.

'The sales of flour at Hakim's mill went up from week to week — and as the needs of the city remained the same, those at Selim's mill declined. It was not long before the excellent Hakim had captured half of Selim's trade.

'But the glories of this world weary me. The noise and numbers of Hakim's new establishment spoiled my repose. My visits grew less frequent; and having obtained from a mutual friend an introduction to Selim, I made myself familiar with his now more humble house, and was charmed to discover a real friend. He was disconsolate, as you may imagine. His income was falling. The demand for his flour, already but a half of its former total, grew less and less. My connection with Hakim's new-found prosperity had been whispered abroad, and, one evening, Selim frankly asked me for aid. "Do not," said he, "betray any secrets; be silent if you will. But should you deign to advise me I would be grateful."

'"It is a small matter," I replied, gently, "and a very simple one. Hakim has made his place of business a Desirable Resort. His guests abound. He naturally receives their orders. You remain as you were and are deserted."

'"You mean," said Selim, anxiously, "that I should use some part of my patrimony to build a Hall of Entertainment, to purchase sherbet and sweetmeats, and to hire a troupe of players!"

'"Undoubtedly," I answered, "but if you only do that you will hardly redress the balance; for the custom of haunting Hakim's mill has grown strong. Come, furnish your place with these things, but add a score of dancing girls, several lions in cages, an elephant and a tamer of serpents!" "It will cost me dear!" said Selim, with hesitation. "You have asked for my advice," I returned, "I may be wrong. It is no affair of mine. But that is my judgment."

'I was not surprised to remark that Selim's establishment within the month had increased by all these things; and one of the lions having eaten its keeper in full sight of the crowd, a multitude nightly besieged the doors of the Western Mill in the hope of further entertainment. Selim's sales rapidly caught up with Hakim's, passed them, and left his rival with but a quarter of his former turnover; while in the city men pointed me out mysteriously as the man whose touch turned all things into gold.

'Hakim, who had treated me a little coldly after my visits to Selim, swallowed his pride, approached me by night and asked me what he should do. "Fireworks," was my natural reply.

'"Alas!" he answered, "I have not the wherewithal! These entertainments are terribly expensive."

'"We must throw minnows to catch whales," I said. "Associate me for a small part in your future gains — or, if you prefer it, give me a lien on your mill — and the fireworks are easily arranged!"

'He preferred a lien on the mill, and the fireworks were certainly magnificent. But when Selim, in his turn, consulted me, I suggested a far nobler display, crowned by the discharge of cannon, which, for a similar (but larger) lien on *his* mill I was happy to provide. Hakim, begging me to observe the most profound secrecy, came to me in disguise and implored my last succor, saying he was a broken man. I have never been deaf to such human appeals.

'"I will not foreclose," said I, "but let me take over your property in partnership with you and I will see what can be done."

'My reputation was by this time such that the suggestion was like a gift of gold. The unhappy Hakim, with sobs shaking his bosom, signed an instrument which made me half owner and sole manager of his business, and patiently awaited the miracle.

'Meanwhile Selim's mill, though now doing four-sixths of the city's grinding, was in difficulties. The fireworks, the lions, the dancing girls (to whom was now added a tank of crocodiles) more than ate up the profits, and their owner, in a fit of despair, urged me to save him in his extremity — but implored me to keep the whole thing a dead secret, lest his credit should suffer. I could not resist his drawn face and broken manner — so different from the placid countenance of old — and I told him, with the ring of real affection in my voice, that he need not fear any insistence on my legal rights, but that, for a half of the profits (so that we should both be interested) I would manage the failing concern.

'If Hakim had sobbed, Selim wept unrestrainedly, and was free to confess that men of my generosity were the emissaries of heaven.

'What followed was indeed extraordinary! I am justly proud of my business sense. None have denied my genius in affairs. Yet somehow or other neither mill could prosper in the months that followed. I was tireless in my efforts. I came daily to the works of each after sunrise, and spent the whole day between the two supervisors, buying corn, selling flour, and fixing prices. I shut down the foolish extravagance of circuses and all that nonsense — which I now clearly saw to be superfluous (since both mills were under one hand); I ruled my servants with severity; I allowed no waste. I kept rigorous accounts. Despite all this, whether because I bought my corn a little too dear, or sold my flour a little too cheap, or allowed Hakim and Selim a little too much money for their private establishments, loss followed loss, and within a year it was patent that both mills must cease their activities or fail to meet the sums owing to the merchants in corn.

'I consulted on the last critical night with my two partners, and we agreed that there was nothing for it but to sell the two places for what they would fetch. I had not been so base as to conceal my losses. My books were open to all; and the offers made were so contemptible that with a sigh I braced myself to my duty and bought in the derelict property with my own remaining coin. They thus fetched not a fiftieth of their original value, but far more than any bidder had proposed to pay; a business losing more and more heavily with every passing day is worthless.

'Hakim and Selim, taking their shares (one-half of the whole, as was but justice), put each his few silver pieces into a dainty moleskin (with which I presented each as a parting gift), and in our last meal together we discoursed upon the Vicissitudes of Human Life and the Fate of the Soul.

'"What is man," said Hakim, "that he should consider wealth? There is but one air to be breathed, which is that of communion with the Divine. I count my worldly loss as nothing. I have here enough, if I live on dry bread, to take me forty days' journey before my coins are exhausted. I will go into the high hills; there I will make my hermitage and pray till death finds me. Especially," said he, turning to me, who sat silent, with my face buried, "will I pray for *you*, my friend, who have so stood by me in good and in ill, and have suffered with me in our last misfortunes."

'Selim was no less moved. "I, for my part," said he, "will travel as a mendicant, praying always as I go from shrine to shrine, and thrice a day remembering *you*, for no other would have stood by us so loyally to the end!"

'They rose to depart and, unable to conceal my deep emotion, I replied in a subdued tone. "My brothers, I am not worthy. I must remain in the world, to live I know not how, by some pursuit, for I am incapable of contemplation; but do you go forth, and never fail in your prayers to weary heaven for the ruined and unhappy Mahmoud."

'We embraced and parted. From that day the tide of my adventure turned. Corn I soon contrived to buy with advantage; flour I sold at quite excellent prices. The accounts balanced; soon they showed a profit. As two mills were superfluous I handed one over to form a delightful resting place for the aged and virtuous of the city; under the proviso, of course, that it should never be used for commerce. One mill had always been enough for the grinding of the city's flour; and with expenses thus lessened I was able to lower the price of bread by three copper pieces the thousand loaves, and yet to leave myself a sufficient, and soon an ample, surplus. Nor was there any place for a rival.

'See, my dear nephews!' said Mahmoud, now raised to enthusiasm, 'how all things work together at last for good! The poor — or, at any rate, the bakers — had flour provided them a trifle cheaper than of old; Hakim and Selim were serving God in silence and joy, far off; the social waste of keeping up a superfluous mill was ended; and I myself was materially rewarded by an increasing fortune.

'If you ask me to what we all in common owed these graces, I might cite my own sobriety, clear thought, loyalty, tenacity, foresight and faith. I do not deny these gifts which have been granted me. But most of all do I ascribe such blessings to the prayers poured out in the distant hermitage, on the remote highways of the world, by Hakim and Selim; for by so much more is the soul stronger than any poor cunning of the mind.

'And this kind of commerce is called, my sweet infants, a MERGER.'

# IN THE RED SEA

### BY MAJOR ARTHUR W. HOWLETT

From the *Manchester Guardian*, September 5
(RADICAL LIBERAL DAILY)

ONE must always respect the Red Sea. Other seas may be placid, remote, even ridiculous. There is the German Ocean, which is not necessarily German, and is certainly not an ocean; and there is the White Sea, which nobody troubles about. But half the keels of the world furrow the Red Sea, and, thanks to Pharaoh, it has a claim even to antiquity.

In these days, too, of compromise and half-measures, one must admire absolutism, if only for its rarity; and the Red Sea holds out no hope of relenting, no relaxation from its immitigable barrenness. It might have been the first thing made before there was such a thing as life, or the last when all life had perished, but it refuses to meet the earth halfway. As it was in the days of the Israelites, so it is now — rocky, stony, arid, grassless, treeless, naught but a mirror from day to day, year in, year out, of the fiercest of suns.

There are eleven hundred odd miles of it from north to south, from the red hills about Suez to the islanded Straits of Bab el Mandeb. Eleven hundred miles of a superfluity of oceanic naughtiness. You may be sure when you enter it it, will show you some of its vagaries. Hence the name of the straits — the Gate of Tears. To me it is inconceivable how mortal men ever endured its frightfulness in slow and often becalmed sailing ships, devoid of fans and ice-machines and all those contrivances which even to-day in fast steamers often fail to save the miserable travelers from heatstroke.

It has happened, when there has been a following wind, that steamships have had to be turned round in order to sail in the face of the breeze and give the occupants air and a brief breathing-spell before resuming their voyage. Again, though landlocked and, to all appearance on the maps, a mere thread of salt water between Asia and Africa, I have known unaccountable great seas get up in it, so that the miserable passenger, besides being prostrated by the heat, is subject to the added miseries of seasickness.

As if all this were not enough, in days not very remote pirates in swift-sailing dhows had their lairs along its rocky coasts, and descended like sea wolves on all who were unable to defend themselves. It lent itself remarkably well to the pastime of walking the plank, for its hot waters teem with all kinds of horrible marine monsters. And if you ever got ashore you would infallibly die of thirst and sunstroke, so that on all counts the hardihood of the ancient voyagers is something to be wondered at.

People who have been in Palestine have often expressed surprise that it could ever have been called the land of milk and honey. It was obviously a matter of contrast. If they had gone on farther south, beyond the Dead Sea to the Sinai Peninsula, they would have understood. People who had wandered long in that region would rave about the fertility and verdure of an Ancoats recreation ground or a Wigan coal-tip. I have lived in the desert for months, and can speak feelingly.

Sinai, of course, forms one boundary of the upper arm of the Red Sea. Somewhere there, on those mistless mountains, so unworn that even yet they stand in countless jagged pinnacles to catch the flaming gold of the desert sunsets, lies the unknown grave of Moses; and day by day the steamers pass, leaving their long plumes of smoke adrift and dipping down in unconscious salutation to the leader of long ago.

It is pitiful to see the children wilt and whiten after even one day of the Red Sea. The decks that were alive with their romps become still, and crusty old Indian colonels — one has to keep up these time-honored expressions of the East — begin to say that there are compensations in the Red Sea, after all. One struggles in vain with collars which turn limp and sodden as they are buttoned. The night brings little respite. The sun literally burns. Every glancing wavelet is like a burning-glass focused on to the eyeballs. Men and women loll about listlessly, counting the days to their escape.

Perhaps the saddest thing of all is the number of invalids who flicker out in these three or four days of the voyage home. Many stay in India just too long, hoping for a little increment of pension to lighten the dull days at home, only to perish at last in this final fiery trial, and, like the dog with the bone, lose all. The whole steamer-track of the Red Sea is one long grave. Were it possible to erect memorials to them, one would see the long line of gray stones standing up above the solemn waters, mile after mile to the horizon, the witnesses of those who had given their lives for India.

One sees land but seldom most of the way; but north and south, where the land closes in, the rocks, like grim red shadows, come down to the sea and anon throw off islands all stark and bald like the motherland, but a little relief to the eye. There are lighthouses perched on some of them, and the passenger who scans their bony framework wonders what the lighthousemen do all day. Some have not even an island to perch on, but rise straight up out of the sea. It is strange to see them grow up into view and slide behind as the great steamer holds on its way with steady muffled thrum! thrum! of the engines and the oily waters feathering sluggishly astern.

When it roughens a little the small silver flying-fish spatter about in shoals, leaping from the wave crests and gliding a hundred yards or so till their wings dry and they drop back into the sea. As you pace the deck by night, after dinner, you behold in the dark mystery which encompasses the lonely vessel plaques of phosphorescence heaving up and down and vanishing into the gloom.

The habit of sleeping on deck, which used to be universal a dozen years ago and less, seems to have lapsed now that the stewards have refused to bring the bales of mattresses and bedding up from below. In the old days a man's cabin number was chalked on the deck, his bed was unrolled beside it, and he there disposed himself for the night. This practice started at Suez and continued all the way to Bombay; and a weird sight it was to see those long rows of sheeted figures lying out on the planking in the dim shadows of the deck lights. A few hardy spirits do it still, but most people now sleep below all the way.

At the bottom end of the Red Sea, where the ship turns the corner to make Aden, the Southern Cross comes into view by night, for this is the farthest south point on the voyage to India. And here just before emergence into the Indian Ocean lies the barren island of Perim. I have watched its fortunes intermittently for fifteen years, and see that it has now grown quite a big boy. With its coal stacks, wharves, and cranes, its huge oil-tanks, and its bungalows and tin sheds, it has become a serious station on the eastward route. Half a dozen vessels lie at anchor before it, grilling in the hot sun. Not a blade of grass is to be seen, only rocks, bare, bare rocks, all a-shimmer in the heat. Hard by are the Twelve Apostles, rocky islets of ill omen with small sandy coves and beaches, and cruel, iron-looking projections on which the spray goes flying heavenward.

The Romance of the Red Sea might well be written: there is plenty of it, most of it rather grim and tragical, it is true, but well worth the recording. To follow the course of one of the pilgrim ships from India to Mecca, or at least to the landfall thereof, is an Odyssey of itself. Where in the West do we find the ecstatic spirit which can lead old men to devote the savings of a lifetime and the last hours of life itself to so immaterial an enterprise? The risks are tremendous — cholera, sunstroke, heat-stroke, shipwreck, exhaustion, all take their toll of the faith-girded Mussulman; but he holds on, never doubting, and dies there, to join his bones with those of thousands more that lie awash in the Red Sea, or else returns to his native land to bear ever more the honorific of 'Pilgrim' (Hadji), and be a sort of Cœur de Lion among his fellow men. You are well out of the Red Sea, but all the while you must acknowledge a certain spell about it if you have a grain of imagination or poetry.

# RADHA'S CHILD

## BY C. R.

[*The modest literary merit of the story we print below is compensated by the light it throws upon one phase of India's struggle for self-redemption — the propaganda against caste. Recently three hundred leading citizens of Surat, breaking through centuries of senseless prejudice against pariahs and lower castemen, publicly repented for their past injustice by volunteering to perform the city's scavenger service — the most conspicuous repudiation of caste possible.*]

From *Young India,* September 28
(Gandhi Weekly)

'I, LEFT my darling in the yard. Apple of my eye! My pearl! I left my child in the yard. Who has carried him away? My pearl! My darling!'

Thus crying aloud and hurrying hither and thither, like one mad, alternately weeping and laughing wildly, Radha searched for her child. She had fondly hoped the child would soon grow to be a man and comfort her in the world which God had made lonely for her all too early in her young life.

'I told you not to put that ill-omened bracelet round his little wrist. Was not your ill-luck enough for us? Ask Lakshmi of the next house whether she has been playing a joke hiding your darling.'

'Oh, the thieves were here yesterday. I suspected the gang even then. I had the child on my arm and they kept staring at the shining gold as I put the rice into their begging bowl.'

Radha's mother was right. A gang of kidnappers had stolen Radha's child for the gold bracelet. From that day Radha was crazy.

It was the Scavengers' Colony.

'Ponnayya, come and see: God has sent us a gift,' said Lakki. And her husband came and saw the wonder. A shining little baby in the dungheap near the wall, just by the prickly-pear bush, and a great big cobra with its hood angrily spread out as if to protect the child from evildoers.

'Don't disturb it. It is a god come with a gift for us.'

But Lakki's entreaty was of no avail. Ponnayya the scavenger went into the house and brought a heavy bamboo stick. The serpent was just moving away into the bush, when a heavy blow on its head despatched it.

'What have you done?' cried Lakki as she picked up the smiling child and suckled it. 'The poor thing is so hungry. You have killed the good snake. Ill luck will surely come of it. Was n't it enough we lost our child?'

Three days afterwards Ponnayya had the smallpox. There was an epidemic in the town, and it was not strange that he caught the disease; but Lakki attributed it to the snake. She made expiatory sacrifices to the stone snakes on the tank-bund. But it was of no avail. Ponnayya died and left Lakki a widow.

Ponnayya left debts. He had been fond of drink, like the other scavengers of the colony, and his wages together with his wife's could not make both ends meet. The money-lender, a Tamil Mussulman, came and worried her and took away the brass pots, pickaxe, shovel and other things of value in the hut, not minding Lakki's imprecations and threats.

However, her wages were increased a little by the Municipal Chairman, who was a kind soul, and indeed financially she was better off widowed than when her drunken husband was alive.

Little Ponna, that was the boy's name, now grew up and was attached to the railway station as a porter-boy. He would bring a couple of annas every day to his mother, who though old still served the Municipality diligently. Ponna was smart and was a favorite with the station staff. But of course he was a pariah boy and could only perform duties permissible for an outcaste.

One day he went into a first-class compartment as the train arrived, along with two other competing porter-boys. The passenger was a Hindu gentleman. He was apparently a high official who would pay liberally. He handed his portmanteau to Ponna. The other boys grew jealous and one of them said, 'Swami! He is a pariah boy.'

'Is it so?' cried the Big One angrily, and plucked the bag back from Ponna and drove him out of the compartment.

Ponna ran away in terror and was too late to find employment that day even among the European passengers.

The Big One stopped at the station master's office and said something about high caste passengers and *Panchama* porters. The station master was apologetic. 'Ponna!' called the station master after the rush was over. 'You ought not to touch a Brahmin's luggage.'

'Sir, don't I know? But the gentleman handed the bag to me himself.'

'Young fellow, you are too handsome and smart-looking, and they don't find out your caste. Don't do it again.' Ponna went to his mother that day empty-handed.

'No luck to-day, mother,' he said, and told what had happened.

'What if we are pariahs, is not our blood red? Have we not the same flesh and the same bones? But why did you go into that man's compartment? Were there no white men in the train?'

'I saw liveried servants and a great crowd near that carriage and I thought it was a white *dorai* inside and went in.'

'Well, never mind, my boy; drink your *kanjee*. God will protect us.'

It was a lucky day for Ponna — he had made double his usual earnings. He ran along the road to his house when he saw some of his fellow-porters standing in front of the coffee shop in the bazaar. He halted and asked for rice-cakes for one anna.

'Swami, he is a pariah boy,' said one of the boys to the Brahmin shopkeeper. 'Get away, you scoundrel. How dare you?' cried the man and Ponna ran away in a fright while the other porter-boys laughed.

He stopped again near a drinking-shop. An old woman had her little basket-stall of cakes and other things at the entrance. He bought an anna's worth and was greedily eating them while still hot. A haggard old man joked the boy, and told him the cake would taste better if he had a drink. The boy hesitated, but another tempter joined. And they went into the saloon together. Ponna went home that day somewhat late.

Lakki died one day, whereupon Ponna (who was a young man now) and his wife had to leave the Municipal Colony. The old woman had saved more than Ponna thought. She spent liberally for the marriage; yet there were Rs. 120, all bright silver, carefully tied in a little bag and hidden in a pot. Ponna wished to open a little grocer's shop with this capital. He could not, of course, find a stall in the regular bazaar. A pariah could not do that, and even if he could get a place for rent there, no one would buy of him. He could open a shop in the pariah quarters, but the business being only among pariahs, would not be much. He finally made up his mind to try a shop in the Paracheri. The problem of buying his stock had to be solved. There was another pariah shopkeeper there, who would not give advice. He was having very little business himself and he felt the new competitor would ruin him quite. Ponna had to buy his goods through an upper caste acquaintance; and between this agent and the *mandiman* his buying prices were so high that his venture did not flourish. Purchasers were few and he lost heavily. Soon his little enterprise failed.

Ponna and his wife then worked in the great spinning and weaving mill in the neighboring city. The wife rose at four every morning to cook their meals in time. A neighbor agreed to keep their child for them when they were at the mill. They paid a part of their earnings for this. They returned home late. Ponna's wife would come earlier and take the child from her friend and make her house ready. But Ponna would come home late, often drunk.

They led a miserable life. Ponna would often think of his mother Lakki, who earned less than he was now earning, yet they had lived so happily and in comfort. Lakki had never uttered one harsh word. But now after the day's toil when he went home there was nothing but anger and complaint awaiting him. He drank more and more heavily.

There was a big meeting in the city. Gandhi's men had come to address the people. Ponna also was there with some other mill-hands. They spoke words which he, too, a Panchama, drunken, illiterate, could understand. 'Do not drink; spin,' they said. 'Do not drive the untouchable away; he too is a brother.'

The vision of his little shop came back to Ponna. 'If I could have had it in the regular bazaar, and could have bought my stock myself and have sold freely to everyone like the others, my mother's money would not have been lost.' So thought Ponna as he dragged himself away from the liquor shop that day without going in.

Ponna in fact was a Brahmin boy, Radha's son, but neither he nor anybody else knew it.

# A PAGE OF VERSE

## THE LATER AUTUMN
### BY THOMAS HARDY
*[Saturday Review]*

No more lovers under the bush
  Stretched at their ease;
  No more bees
Tangling themselves in your hair as
    they rush
  On the line of your track
  Leg-laden, back
  With a dip to their hive
  In a prepossessed dive.

Toadsmeat is mangy, frosted, and sere;
  Apples in grass
  Crunch as we pass,
And rot ere the men who make cider
    appear.
  Couch-fires abound
  On fallows around,
  And shadows extend
  Like lives soon to end.

Spinning leaves join the remains shrunk
    and brown
  Of last year's display
  That lie wasting away,
On whose corpses they earlier as scorn-
    ers gazed down
  From their aëry green height:
  Now in the same plight
  They huddle; while yon
  A robin looks on.

## AFTER VICTOR HUGO
### BY WILFRID THORLEY
*[New Witness]*

CLIMB, squirrel, climb the tall oak tree
To where the last sprays dizzily
  Lean out and tremble, reedy-soft!
Fly, doting stork, that still dost dwell
Beside thine ancient pinnacle
From spire to rampart and the fell
  Height of the frowning keep aloft!

Old eagle, quit thy cleft and ride
Above thine ancient hills that hide
  In raiment of eternal ice!
Low-nested bird whose songs begin
When dawn first brings the daylight in,
Fly upward with thy happy din,
  O lark, to gates of paradise!

Gaze from thy tree, or mime the moon
From topmost towers of marble hewn,
  High tor or heaven! Seest thou then
Horizon-far through mist the pale
Glint of helm-feathers on the mail
Or shod-hooves beating like a flail
  To bring my lover home agen?

## LOVER'S REPLY TO GOOD ADVICE
### BY RICHARD HUGHES
*[Spectator]*

COULD you bid an acorn
When in earth it heaves
On Time's backward wing be borne
To forgotten leaves:
Could you quiet Noah's Flood
To an essence rare,
Or bid the roaring wind
Confine in his lair:

Could round iron shell
When the spark was in it
Hold powder so well
That it never split:
Had you reins for the sun,
And curb, and spur,
Held you God in a net
So He might not stir:

Then might you take this thing,
Then strangle it, kill!
By weighing, considering,
Conform it to will!
Like Christ's Self contemn it,
Revile, mock, betray:
But being Seed — Wind — God —
It bears all away!

# LIFE, LETTERS, AND THE ARTS

## A NONSENSE LIBRARY AND OTHER LIBRARIES

EVERY good book-collector has his own particular hobby — one kind of book upon which he dotes beyond all others. O'Crœsus, the paint millionaire, is given to the assembling of Elizabethan quartos, and Van Crassus, the noted dealer in pig iron, has a fondness for Elzevirs and Aldines, while McMidas is no more celebrated for his operations in high finance than for the relentless ferocity and the limitless expanse of purse wherewith his agents follow up every really good sale of autographed first editions of modern authors. (McMidas is English in his taste; modern authors are a recent London fad.)

Alas, these wealthy gentlemen, having first acquired most of the paint, pig iron, and dollars in the world, have drawn to themselves too many of the best books as well; and though even book-collecting millionaires die in time, they have a way of willing their choicest acquisitions to endowed libraries, universities, and public institutions of one kind and another — where, no doubt, they mightily rejoice the souls of the elaborately erudite custodian who dusts them and of the poor student who flattens his nose against their glass cases, — but whence they emerge not again to the salesroom, and where they sniff never more the dusty battles of the auction. Rare books are no longer for the impecunious.

No sooner does some thoughtful bibliophile invent a hobby and joyously bestride it, than he finds his hobby become famous, and the millionaires are upon him. Up go the prices! Away go the books! Pass fifty years; wills begin to go to probate, and the librarians chuckle gleefully as first editions of the *Pickwick Papers* — in parts, complete — Folios with the Droeshout plate in various stages, Breeches Bibles, and other books, with rare and quaint and curious errors and inscriptions and associations, fall into their unrelaxing grasp.

There was a time when First Folios were to be had by any Londoner. The Bodleian Library casually disposed of its copy, only to buy it back for thousands a century or two later. The Spanish censor at Valladolid had no scruples about tearing out a whole play (it makes one shiver to hear — even with the mind's ear — the ripping of those precious pages); and in Queen Bess's day the booksellers about 'Powle's' probably felt no special emotion in the presence of a quarto that is rare and precious now. Charles Lamb — no millionaire, certainly — had his fill of them, and Coleridge languidly waved off several thousand pounds rather than forego the delights of 'lazy reading of old folios.' But into this paradise of cheap collecting came the serpent in the form of the wealthy collector.

There was once a happy time — not very long ago — when the first editions of modern authors, too, sold for the prices their publishers fixed, never dreaming of the struggles of dealers and collectors over those selfsame volumes a few scant years later. But first editions of Wells and Moore, of Masefield and Conrad, are not for the poor man nowadays. Mr. Wells is probably wealthy enough to buy a collection of his own first editions, but not every famous English author can indulge himself in his own works. McMidas and O'Crœsus are at it again.

Rare books and first editions are too expensive. What we want is a new hobby. We have New Thought, the New Education, the New Heredity, the New Psychology — why not the New Bibliomania? Why not the Library of Nonsense? The Philistines aver that all libraries are nonsense — let us have one library at least that is *intended* to be all nonsense. Though literature is not nonsense, some nonsense is undeniably literature. What hobby more agreeable than collecting it?

Let us have our nonsense libraries, by all means, or at least a nonsense shelf. Here the *Bab Ballads* (an edition without Gilbert's own drawings is worthless) may jostle Alice, astray forever amid the quips and quiddities of Wonderland. Here, too, the strange plants and the astounding animals and the meaningless, musical verses of Edward Lear shall stand close beside them, for the joy of all good souls who know better than to look in the dictionary for *runcible* — that admirable adjective, that worthy companion to Lewis Carroll's immortal inventions, *frumious* and *tulgy*.

If we admit Americans to the nonsense shelves, we shall have to include Mr. Burgess and Mr. Herford, Mr. Tudor Jenks and Miss Carolyn Wells. Whatever we may choose from among the modern Englishmen, we must have all three of those chuckleful books that Hilaire Belloc writes when he is neither belaboring a bogy labeled 'Modern Thought,' nor riding Pegasus to hounds, nor even quarrelling with Mr. Wells. We must have Mr. Belloc in the mood of *The Bad Child's Book of Beasts*, *More Beasts for Worse Children*, and *Cautionary Tales*.

These are the nucleus of the Nonsense Library; and — as the true collector is ready to be off to the ends of the earth when rarities are to be picked up — so we shall scan the bookstalls and the publishers' announcements for nonsense. I suspect we shall find a good deal of it. Not the kind of nonsense we want, perhaps, for nonsense books are less frequent than books in which the sense is present but not very apparent.

Absolute nonsense is a rarity, rare as absolute beauty, absolute poetry, absolute music. Not quite so precious. Not a triple distillation of the human spirit — no, no, of course not. But delectable and delightful, all the same.

> They told me you had been to her,
> And mentioned me to him;
> She gave me a good character,
> But said I could not swim.

That is quite perfect of its sort, though it is a perfection very different from

> Charm'd magic casements, opening on the foam
> Of perilous seas, in faery lands forlorn.

Pure nonsense, the one; pure poetry, the other. And who, having the capacity to appreciate poetry, will despise nonsense?

✤

'L'ÉCHO DE FRANCE'

*L'Écho de France*, as befits its name, is appearing in London instead of Paris; for the echo is intended to be heard by the ears of little Britishers who are studying the language of the other side of the Channel. What a jolly time the modern infant must have in the British Isles. No more dull 'texts,' apparently. Instead this wellprinted and divertingly illustrated little French paper, which appears weekly — four pages for a penny — reproduces jokes from the French comic papers (discreetly selected, needless to say), prints interesting but simple articles on French life, and adds to its other attractions the adventures of 'Hippolyte and Hegesippe,' which no normal child is likely to scorn.

Hippolyte and Hegesippe are two French provincials. They visit Paris, and their predicaments are made diverting to the extent of half a column every week, with an amusing set of drawings which have the characteristic deft touch of the French artist in black and white. Hippolyte and Hegesippe visiting the Louvre and falling foul of an artist, Hippolyte and Hegesippe ordering *bouillabaisse* and *moules au lait* to the mute horror of a metropolitan waiter — the adventures of this guileless pair render education as nearly painless as it can be.

While two French papers for Engglish students are being printed — for *L'Écho de France* is merely a companion to *La France*, a summary of the French press issued by the same firm of English publishers — a group of Englishmen in Paris are bringing out a fortnightly English paper. This is to be called *The Briton*, and will be edited for children and older persons who are studying the English language.

✣

### VERGIL'S FARM

WAS the farm on which P. Vergilius Maro spent his boyhood at the modern Pietola or at the modern Calvisano? The former is the traditional site, but archæological studies recently made by Mr. G. E. K. Braunholtz, Senior Classical Lecturer in the University of Manchester, lead him to favor the latter.

For the first thirty years of his life, Vergil dwelt in the village of Andes, and it is the simple life of the Roman countryside there that he describes in the *Eclogues*. The scholar Probus, who may very likely have got his information from Vergil himself, says that the village lay thirty Roman miles — twenty-two English miles — from Mantua. This is all we really know about the location of Andes, which vanished long ago.

A tradition that is at least as old as Dante placed the site at Pietola, a hamlet lying about two miles south-east of Mantua, but its position cannot be reconciled with Probus's statement. Mommsen found this fact sufficient reason for rejecting Pietola, but he did not attempt to suggest any new site.

Mr. Braunholtz, however, offers several bits of evidence that seem fairly conclusive — which is, after all, about as close to proof as one is likely to get in a question of this sort. He finds that two inscriptions, probably dating from the first century of the Empire, were set up by members of the Vergilian and Magian houses — those of the poet's father and mother respectively — in two villages near Pietola. One of these villages is Calvisano, which lies exactly thirty Roman miles from Mantua, a little west of the road to Brescia in the southerly foothills of the Alps. The Calvisano inscription is due to a lady whose name was Vergilia and who belonged to the poet's family. Obviously, then, the poet's family was established in the vicinity.

Armed with these facts, Mr. Braunholtz set about making comparisons between the scenery at Calvisano and the descriptions of the countryside in the five local *Eclogues*. The scenery at Pietola is wholly different. That at Calvisano corresponds closely. Most remarkable of all is a low ridge which bounds the eastern horizon, and 'sinks gently into the plain,' precisely as Vergil describes. Many a ridge in northern Italy sinks gently into the plain, to be sure, but no other is situated at precisely the right distance from Mantua according to Probus's description. From Pietola nothing can be seen but fields, dykes, and marshes; but from Calvisano the Alps are in full view. Mr. Braunholtz may not have proved his case, but he has at least made it as probable as any one is likely to do.

✣

THE RUBAIYAT OF TWO MODERN OMARS

PERSIA, once the home of Omar Khayyám, most bibulous of poets, has climbed unsteadily on the water wagon. Mohammedan countries are nominally dry, for liquor of any form is forbidden to the good Moslem. But Persia is a land dominated by the Shiite sect, whom the more powerful Sunnites regard as unorthodox; and though the most rigid followers of the Prophet glanced askance at Omar even in his own day, only now have the protests of the *Ulema* or holy men compelled the government to enforce the Prophet's teaching with regard to strong drink.

Two British voices are raised in the *rubai'y* stanza that Edward Fitzgerald's translation of Omar made famous and familiar in English-speaking lands, to wail the passing of the grape. Their choice of form is appropriate, but it is amusing to recall that a strictly respectable Persian family would hardly regard Omar's *Rubaiyat* as fit reading. It is as a writer of learned mathematical treatises that he is praised in his own land.

The *Westminster Gazette* thus greets the news from Teheran: —

The Moving Finger writes; and on the Scroll
An awful Legend sears the Poet's Soul
   And spells his doom: 'This Caravanserai
Will be, henceforward, under State Control.'

Perchance with Pitfall, but no more with Gin,
The Road's beset that we may wander in,
   And he whose Muse is nourished by the Vine
Will find his Inspiration growing thin!

The Tavern Door no longer is agape,
And if there should appear an Angel Shape
   It can be only that of Pussyfoot
With Something substituted for the Grape!

Come, then, Omar, with me into the Shade —
The Loaf, the Book of Verse, may be mislaid,
   But we will seek what Solace may be found
Held captive in a Jug of Lemonade!

'Lucio,' of the *Manchester Guardian*, is likewise inspired, and he, too, chooses Omar's *rubai'y* stanza, to lament the downfall of the wine he loved: —

Dreaming when Dawn's Left Hand was in the Sky,
I heard a Voice within the Tavern cry,
   'Awake, my Little Ones, and fill the Cup
Before Life's Liquor — and our Land — be dry.'

They say the Sleuth and Pussyfoot now keep
The Courts where Jamshyd gloried and drank deep:
   And Bahram, that great Hunter — he now stalks
The Bootleggers that o'er the Frontier creep.

Iram indeed is gone with all its Rose,
And now the Grape must follow, I suppose:
   Why, even Mere Amusement gets the Bird —
My Hat, this is the Gloomiest of Shows!

But come with old Khayyám and leave the Drys
To run the Show as seems to Them most wise:
   One Thing is certain — there are Other Lands
In which the Vintner still his Juice supplies.

With me to some more friendly Haven blown
Retire to call your Soul (and Throat) your Own —
   Where Norma Talmadge dines with London's Mayor
And Entertainment claims its rightful Throne.

Or stay behind: and when Thyself shall pass
With Sobered Foot where, scattered on the Grass,
   I kept my famous Loaf and Flask of Wine,
Turn down that now forever Empty Glass!

# BOOKS ABROAD

**Old Diplomacy and New, 1876–1922,** by A. L. Kennedy. London: John Murray, 1922. 18s.

*[Daily Telegraph]*

MR. A. L. KENNEDY, the author of this volume, is a son and grandson of distinguished members of the Diplomatic Service, and he himself is a student of foreign affairs who has traveled all over Europe as a representative of the Foreign Department of the *Times*. He is consequently in an exceptional position to reveal the inner meaning of the transition from the late Lord Salisbury to Mr. Lloyd George, and to judge between the secret diplomacy of the past and the 'diplomacy by conference' of to-day.

In his introduction, Sir Valentine Chirol points out that the Berlin Congress was in actual fact the last great European Congress on the old model; but between that congress and the open diplomacy of this century there has been an intricate evolution, which this volume interprets with extreme lucidity. The student of international politics will welcome the book as even in tone, broad-minded, and coldly sagacious. The general reader will enjoy it for its many side lights into the calculated obscurities of European chanceries.

**The Church of the Holy Sepulchre,** by the Reverend H. T. F. Duckworth. London: Hodder and Stoughton, 1922. 10s. 6d.

*[Westminster Gazette]*

BY a natural impulse, there is no end to the effort to restore at any rate an approximate probability to the ascriptions of the sites. The latest is Mr. Duckworth's book. Architecturally, all his ground had, as he admits, been covered by Mr. Jeffrey's published work, though the latter's completed volume on the Holy Sepulchre apparently had not been separately published when the materials for Mr. Duckworth's book were compiled. Topographically, he expresses opinion and adduces no proof.

Indeed, he could not. The main problem of *The Church of the Holy Sepulchre* is whether or not the original building of Constantine, of which this is the successor, enclosed the veritable sites of the Resurrection and the Crucifixion. Mr. Duckworth urges the unlikelihood of Christian piety and tradition having forgotten the exact sites in three hundred years. Assuming that he is right in his conclusions as to their position in relation to the city walls, there is still, unfortunately, no satisfactory evidence as to their exact correspondence with the events they commemorated. . . .

'Somewhere in the area occupied by the buildings collectively known as "the Church of the Holy Sepulchre," the Crucifixion and the Resurrection took place.' That is Mr. Duckworth's conclusion. Whether or not it is satisfactory each reader must decide, but it is not what the Constantinian Bishop Macarius said, and in the eyes of many it will damage the sacred rocks far more than Persian or Arab or other infidel ever dared.

**Notable Londoners.** London: London Publishing Company, 1922.

*[Westminster Gazette]*

*Notable Londoners*, the first edition of an illustrated *Who's Who*, published by the London Publishing Agency, has many claims to interest and usefulness. Particularly the publication deals with the professional and business, rather than with the social, side of London life.

The large number of people dealt with are widely representative of the everyday professional, financial, commercial, and business life of the city; and the general arrangement of the names and the system of grouping would make reference an easy matter even were the volume not provided with a good index.

It is scarcely necessary to particularize in regard to the contents. Short accounts of well-known figures in every branch of work will be found in the pages. The biographical details of this large number of prominent men are interesting and useful for purposes of reference, and the choice has been well made. There is a photographic reproduction in each case.

**A Hundred Poems,** by Sir William Watson, selected from his various volumes. London: Hodder and Stoughton, 1922. 10s. 6d.

*[Times]*

HERE are one hundred of Sir William Watson's poems, drawn from seventeen volumes, and the selection therefore supersedes the earlier selection, which was made from only six separate books.

The longer narrative poems have been excluded, and so have those which in the narrower sense are political; but the hundred here undoubtedly include the poet's best work in many moods. Were there no others, they would probably afford posterity an all-sufficing indication of his style, gifts, and philosophy. Most poets survive ultimately in a residue, and even if time eliminates a good many pieces in this volume, there ought still to be enough to reward the devotion of any poet's lifetime.

**The Triumph of the Tramp Ship,** by Archibald Hurd. London: Cassell, 1922. 7s. 6d.

[*Times*]

JUST as Mr. Archibald Hurd in *The Sea Traders* brought out the romance of the British mercantile marine by showing how it had been developed by the courage and resource of individual pioneers, so now in this companion volume he traces the history of the cargo-tramp and its influence in promoting the spread of civilization in all lands and in all ages. It is a tremendous theme, but Mr. Hurd accomplishes his task with ease.

Where facts are nonexistent he can be picturesque, if merely conjectural — as, for instance:—
'When the first hunter, pricked by the necessity of obtaining food, or fired by the chase and his own natural curiosity, crossed a river on a fallen tree-limb or a bundle of dry leaves, propelled by himself, the tramp-ship came to birth and entered the service of man.'

**The Life of Jameson,** by Ian Colvin. London: Edward Arnold, 1922. 2 vols. 32s.

[Henry W. Nevinson in the *Manchester Guardian*]

IN these two intensely interesting and well-written volumes Mr. Colvin stirs up again the passions that set this country ablaze a generation ago. I am not sure whether, in Horatian phrase, he is treading a crust of treacherous ash which skims over volcanic fires; one can only hope the fires are at last extinguished. But all who lived through that terrible time will feel once more the heat of the flames.

When the national spirit is roused to the point of war, lies are always in demand. We call them propaganda now. People long to be deceived, and deceived they are. But, until 1914, I can hardly suppose greater lies were ever accepted, even about Napoleon, than during the contest with the South African Republics. 'There were girls in the Gold-reef City!' shrieked the Poet Laureate, glorifying the Jameson Raid. 'We seek no territory, we seek no goldmines!' cried the Prime Minister. South Africans may well have laughed, but the British people loved to believe it. Like Mr. Colvin, they were ready to place Jameson on the same level as Drake and Clive and Wolfe. 'Not once nor twice in our rough island story!'

They saw nothing exaggerated or unnatural in the purpose thus expressed by Cecil Rhodes: 'The furtherance of the British Empire for the bringing of the whole uncivilized world under British rule, for the recovery of the United States, for the making of the Anglo-Saxon race but one Empire.'

Jameson's friend and biographer writes in the same spirit; he could not well have written in any other. Rhodes and Jameson are, naturally, the two gods of his idolatry.

✤

BOOKS ANNOUNCED

COLYER, W. T. *Americanism, a World Menace.* London: Labor Publishing Company. Mr. Colyer proposes a complete exposé of these United States. It is based on seven years acquaintance with America — not too long a time for the purpose, for the United States is a rather large country.

HOUSMAN, LAURENCE. *False Premises.* Oxford: Basil Blackwell, 1922. 3s. 6d. One of a series of plays to be printed under the direction of Mr. B. H. Newdigate. Others will be *The Man Who Ate the Popomack,* by W. J. Turner, *Up-Stream,* by Clifford Bax, and *Advertising, or the Girl Who Made the Sun Jealous,* by Herbert Farjeon and Horace Hornsell. A limited and numbered edition, each signed by the author, will be published at 10s. 6d.

LANE, MRS. ROSE WILDER. *The Peaks of Shala.* London: Chapman and Dodd, 1922. For immediate publication. Describes the author's wanderings among the hill tribes of Albania.

RUTTER, FRANK. *Some Contemporary Artists.* London: Leonard Parsons. Mr. Rutter is a well-known English critic, familiar with the personalities of the artists he discusses, as well as with their work. Among the artists of whom he writes are Sir William Orpen, Augustus John, Walter Sickert, William Rothenstein, Wyndham Lewis, C. R. W. Nevinson, and others of the younger generation.

BOTTOMLEY, GORDON. *A Vision of Giorgione: Three Variations on a Venetian Theme.* London: Constable. These three eclogues will appear in one volume, of which there will be fifty signed copies. The first has not appeared in Great Britain hitherto; the others are revived from the *Gate of Smaragdus.*

GIBSON, ASHLEY. *Cinnamon and Frangipani.* London: Chapman and Dodd. A new book on Ceylon for early publication.

✤

BOOKS MENTIONED

BELLOC, HILAIRE. *The Mercy of Allah.* New York: D. Appleton & Co., 1922. $2.00.
BELLOC, HILAIRE. *More Beasts for Worse Children.* New York: Knopf. $1.25.

# ATLANTIC TEXTS
*Textbooks in Library Form*

### FAMOUS STORIES BY FAMOUS AUTHORS
*Edited by* NORMA H. DEMING *and* KATHERINE I. BEMIS *of the Minneapolis Public Schools*
These stories of great and vital interest to young people have all been most carefully selected and most admirably edited for junior high school use. $1.25

### THE LITTLE GRAMMAR
*By* E. A. CROSS, *Dean of Colorado State Teachers College,* has in a slender volume concentrated all the grammatical principles necessary for the ordinary demands of students. The book is designed especially for the seventh grade. $0.90

### STORY, ESSAY, AND VERSE
*Edited by* CHARLES SWAIN THOMAS *and* HARRY G. PAUL
An anthology of selections from the files of the *Atlantic Monthly*, designed for colleges and senior high schools. $1.50

### THE ATLANTIC BOOK OF MODERN PLAYS
*Edited by* STERLING A. LEONARD *of the University of Wisconsin*
The best of modern drama is represented in this carefully selected volume. The names of Dunsany, Yeats, Synge, Lady Gregory, Galsworthy, indicate somewhat the consistent merit of the collection. $1.50

*Special Rates to Schools*

## THE · ATLANTIC MONTHLY PRESS
8 Arlington Street            Boston (17), Mass.

# THE YALE REVIEW

*Edited by* WILBUR CROSS

*A National Quarterly*

JANUARY, 1923

| | |
|---|---:|
| ALLIES IN PEACE | *Agnes Repplier* |
| IDEALS AND DAY-DREAMS | *Kenneth Grahame* |
| THE MAKING OF TARIFFS | *W. S. Culbertson* |
| MODERN BARBARIANS | *Wilbur C. Abbott* |
| AND SO, I THINK, DIOGENES | *Amy Lowell* |
| SCIENCE AND THE SOUL | *Vernon Kellogg* |
| THE RECALL TO THEOLOGY | *Francis G. Peabody* |
| AUSTRIA AND CENTRAL EUROPE | *Josef Redlich* |
| THE NEAR EAST TANGLE | *Duncan B. Macdonald* |
| LISPET, LISPETT & VAINE | *Walter de la Mare* |

Among the New Books
Letters and Comment

*This Number Free with a New Subscription*

The *Yale Review* is published October, January, April, July
$4.00 a year       $1.00 a single copy

------------------------------------------

The Yale Review,
   120 High St., New Haven, Conn.

Please send me The Yale Review for one year, January number FREE, for which I enclose $4.00.

Name_____

L.A. 12-16-22        Address_____

CPSIA information can be obtained
at www.ICGtesting.com
Printed in the USA
BVHW061544180219
540525BV00013B/567/P

# THE
# YALE
# REVIEW

*Edited by* WILBUR CROSS

*A National Quarterly*

## JANUARY, 1923

ALLIES IN PEACE — *Agnes Repplier*
IDEALS AND DAY-DREAMS — *Kenneth Grahame*
THE MAKING OF TARIFFS — *W. S. Culbertson*
MODERN BARBARIANS — *Wilbur C. Abbott*
AND SO, I THINK, DIOGENES — *Amy Lowell*
SCIENCE AND THE SOUL — *Vernon Kellogg*
THE RECALL TO THEOLOGY — *Francis G. Peabody*
AUSTRIA AND CENTRAL EUROPE — *Josef Redlich*
THE NEAR EAST TANGLE — *Duncan B. Macdonald*
LISPETT & VAINE — *Walter de la Mare*
Among the New Books
Letters and Comment

*This Number Free with a N...*
*The Yale Review* is published October,...
$4.00 a year      $1.00 a su...

---

The Yale Review,
120 High St., New Haven, Conn.

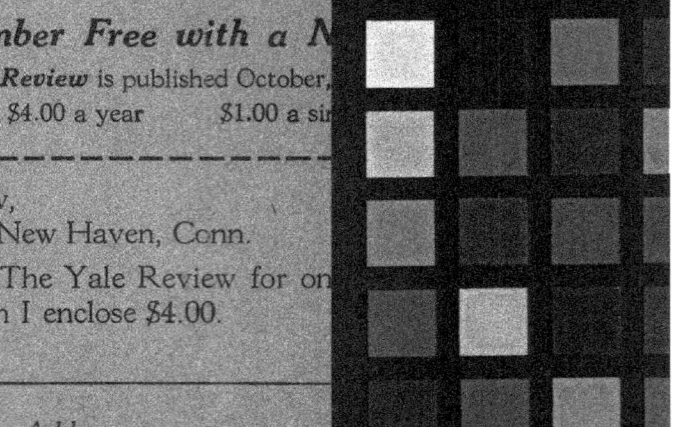

Please send me The Yale Review for on[e]
FREE, for which I enclose $4.00.

*Name* _____

*Address* _____

L.A. 12-16-22